STEM and the City

STEM and the City

A Report on STEM Education in the Great American Urban Public School System

Clair Berube
Virginia Wesleyan University

SueAnne McKinney
Old Dominion University

United Kingdom – North America – Japan – India – Malaysia – China

Emerald Publishing Limited

Emerald Publishing, Floor 5, Northspring, 21-23 Wellington Street, Leeds LS1 4DL

First edition 2025

Copyright © 2025 Clair Berube and SueAnne McKinney. Published under exclusive licence by Emerald Publishing Limited.

Reprints and permissions service Contact: www.copyright.com

No part of this book may be reproduced, stored in a retrieval system, transmitted in any form or by any means electronic, mechanical, photocopying, recording or otherwise without either the prior written permission of the publisher or a licence permitting restricted copying issued in the UK by The Copyright Licensing Agency and in the USA by The Copyright Clearance Center. Any opinions expressed in the chapters are those of the authors. Whilst Emerald makes every effort to ensure the quality and accuracy of its content, Emerald makes no representation implied or otherwise, as to the chapters' suitability and application and disclaims any warranties, express or implied, to their use.

British Library Cataloguing in Publication Data

A catalogue record for this book is available from the British Library

978-1-83708-539-2 (Print paperback)
978-1-83708-538-5 (Print hardcover)
978-1-83708-540-8 (E-Book)

*For our math and science students over the years;
whether they were public school children or past and current college students.
It has been our honor to teach you the beauty of math, science, and foundations
of American education. And for K–12 children all over the United States
who didn't think STEM was for them: This book is for you.*

RIP Dr. Sue McKinney
1960–2024

Contents

Introduction xi
Preface xvii

1 **The History of STEM in American Public Schools** 1
    Emergence of Science as a Separate Subject 7
    Engineering and Technology for Everyone 8

2 **American Anti-Intellectualism, Religion, and the Science Classroom: Culture War of the Worlds** 11
    Anti-Intellectualism and American Society 12
    Race 17

3 **The Pedagogy of Poverty vs. Real STEM Teaching in Urban, High Poverty Schools** 21
    The Pedagogy of Poverty 24
    Exceptional STEM Teachers or "Stars" 24

4 **Gender Bias in STEM Education** 31
    Women and Higher Education 32
    The Importance of Role Models and Mentors 34
    Identity and Science 37
    Slowing Down Scientific Progress 41
    Connections 43
    Einstein's Brain 43

viii • Contents

5 The Effects of No Child Left Behind and High-Stakes Testing on STEM Education 47
    High-Stakes Tests 48
    The Politics of Science Education 49
    The Effects of High-Stakes Testing on Minorities 52
    NCLB and the Poorest of the Poor Minority Urban Students 53
    National Assessment of Educational Progress 53
    PISA 56
    Obama and Race to the Top 59
    The Privatization of Public Schools 61
    Choice and Charter Schools 62
    Neighborhood School Killer 64
    Segregation in Charter Schools 66
    STEM and NCLB 66
    Has NCLB Neglected Gifted Students? 67

6 What Effective STEM Teaching Looks Like 71
    Problem-Based Learning 72
    Creativity 72
    PBL and Creativity 74
    Problem-Based Learning Template 74
    Problem-Solving Cycle for Teachers 75
    Sample Health-Related Problem and Scenario Designed
        by Teachers 75
    Sample Earth Science-Related Problem and Scenario Created
        by Teachers 78
    What Every Teacher Should Know About Physics but Is Afraid
        to Ask 80

7 Educational Malpractice and the Mishandling of STEM Education Pre- and Post-Pandemic 85
    Sueanne E. McKinney and Kala Burrell-Craft
    Challenges Pre and Post Pandemic 87
    The Impact of the Pandemic on STEM Education 89
    Revitalizing the Spark for STEM Education for Urban Learners 92

8 Conclusion: The Future of American STEM Education 95
    Solutions 101
    Parents Rights? 103

References..107

**Appendix: Notes Concerning the Teaching of Physics
to Elementary/Secondary Students**...123
    Reading List 124
    Websites 124
    Videos 125

About the Author, Co-Author, and Contributor..........................127

Introduction

It's January 25, 2021 and the COVID-19 pandemic is still raging. Millions of American parents are confused and panicky about how to help their children navigate the new world of online learning. Many of them are working full time and with day care centers closed as well, they are scrambling to help their children with the classwork that they feel inadequate to teach. As a mother of a then high schooler with autism, I too was trying to navigate this new reality. As a teacher educator and a strong defender of teachers, I (Berube) wrote an op-ed called "Teaching Earns Appreciation in the Pandemic" in the *Virginian-Pilot* newspaper. It had been called "There's a Reason you Suck at Home Schooling" but I figured the local newspaper wouldn't like that title. What I have here is the longer, unedited version.

Parents of America I have good news for you: you are not alone. You are not the only parents in the world today who feel woefully inadequate in the home-schooling of your spawn. Hundreds of millions of parents are coming to this realization almost at once; as you try to create a science fair in your kitchen, or a fractal tetrahedron tower in your den, or a challenge course in your backyard. There is a reason you are struggling, and it has nothing to do with how inept you are, or how brilliant you are in architecture or law or plumbing, or how lazy you are, or how incompetent you are, or how busy you are, or even how drunk you may be (#daydrinking). The reason you are struggling with the education of your home-schooled children is because... EDUCATION IS A PROFESSION!

As shocking and obvious as that statement seems, the reality is sinking in across the globe that teaching is an important profession. Just like medical doctors, who take courses in anatomy, organic and biochemistry, physics, and biology, so too do education majors take major specific courses. I know that we all "know" this so to speak, but we don't all "realize" it. Teacher education departments in universities and colleges across America require students to take any number of content area courses (sciences, history and social studies, English, foreign language, psychology, human growth and development, mathematics); methods courses (science education, language arts education, mathematics education, social studies education, etc.); pedagogy courses (best practices, classroom management, teacher education research, classroom organization, educational technology); and the like. In many of these courses there are cross-cutting themes that appear in all content, including differentiating instruction, technology and culturally relevant pedagogy. At the master's level there are courses such as research methods where teachers learn about T-Tests and ANOVAs and how to conduct action and quasi-experimental research in their own classes. Teachers know how to write complicated lesson plans to the extent that they know how to actually use Bloom's taxonomy to turn what they want your child to do into a daily objective that is measurable and observable. They know how to assess that objective, and they know how to teach the objective at several different levels of learning... all the way from memorization to comprehension to application and evaluation. And just like a medical doctor who knows how to prescribe a different drug if the one you are on isn't working, a teacher knows how to prescribe pedagogical practices to fit the needs of your child.

It is quite humorous to me, a former schoolteacher who now prepares future teachers at the college level, as I watch this realization unfold in household after household, while watching the funny YouTube videos of families struggling to educate their kids without expelling them from the house. We educators have known this for a long time: We are not the slackers society thinks we are; laying on the beach all summer while you schlubs work 9–5. We are not majoring in education because we couldn't cut anything else. We majored in education because we know serious content and we know how to get people to understand it which is no small feat.

One of the most amazing observations from an educator's perch during this pandemic is that society is actually coming to this realization. I mean, if you developed a brain aneurism tomorrow, would you try to get your husband to "home-doctor" it? Lay you on the kitchen table and get out the new set of Wusthof's? Of course not. And hubby (or wife to be gender fair)... you would not feel like a loser either if you knew you couldn't operate on your wife's brain. So why is everyone feeling like they are failing their kids? Why? Because subconsciously after decades and centuries we have been conditioned to think that teaching is so easy that anyone could do it. Or maybe because most teachers are women there is a lack of respect for that reason. Society has "told" us for decades what things women do are not important, are easy or are not complicated. People that work with children don't need to know much at all. Maybe most of us still have this subconscious script running in our brain software. Or maybe . . . fill in the blank.

Teachers also need certain personality traits in order to be any good. They have to be patient, persistent and have a sense of humor. They need to be determined with your unmotivated child and they have to be supportive of your overachiever. They need to be a trusted source of information and they need to model the behavior they wish to elicit from their students. They need to be good writers because they are writing papers for presentations at conferences and articles for publication in scholarly journals. They are applying those research courses they took at the master's level and are using their classrooms to figure out which lessons work and which ones don't, which practices work and which don't and which battles to lose in order to win the war. They also need to be a little bit of a rebel because they need to care more about your individual child, than they care about that rule that threatens to derail their education and in doing so, their very future.

Teachers are so smart. They need to be quick on their feet and they need to be able to connect seemingly unrelated pieces of information so that your child can have that "aha" moment that changes their life forever and that they remember 30 years later as they tell their grandchildren about that moment over beers at a beach fire pit at sunset.

Teachers love your kids. Even if they don't like them sometimes. They don't judge them, in fact they "see" them as fully formed self-actualized people and they know how to get them from where they are now to where their fully formed self is waiting for them. They don't judge the kid who has old clothes or who lacks the newest iPhone . . . just as they also don't judge the more affluent kid with the perfect hairdo and expensive trinkets Mom and Dad bought for them.

It takes a lot of intelligence and schooling to be a good teacher. Teachers have to be constantly reading the latest books and articles in their field. They have to read the newspaper/news outlets and keep up with what is going on in the world, because literally everything going on in the world can be used in a lesson plan.

On a more serious note, some kids however, like my son John who has autism, are really in crisis mode. Unlike regular education students, he cannot do virtual school, which means that legally, he is not getting anything at all. What are school divisions going to do about special ed kids? John is in a self-contained class for kids with autism in a public high school. The class is very small and is staffed by one teacher and two aids. With everyone else staying home in the fall why couldn't special ed kids go to school under careful consideration? Could they be COVID-19 tested along with teachers? What is going to happen to these kids? How are they going to get educated? Are special ed kids the collateral damage society is telling us we have to accept from having to home-school?

As for you parents of regular education students, you are all doing the best you can in this temporary crisis situation. Your kids will survive. Show them love and patience and grace under pressure, and they will learn that lesson for life. But go easy on yourself. Don't lose sleep if your kids are a few minutes behind in their calculus. They'll live and they'll catch up. Remember...no one expects you to be proficient in a whole other profession that takes a master's degree to achieve. But again, kids like my son may never catch up to where they were. I know one thing for sure: we are all stressed out.

So that's the reason you suck at homeschooling. There is a silver lining here: The whole world is finally starting to appreciate the teaching profession. Those of us in schools and colleges of education across America have known this for a long time. Teaching is a high-level profession not to be taken lightly. Teachers need respect and salaries to match. So, parents, relax and thank a teacher!

—**Clair Berube**
Virginia Wesleyan University

* * *

The introduction above was from a draft of an article I had published in the *Virginian-Pilot* on January 5, 2021 as "Teaching earns appreciation in the pandemic." Looking back, we now know that some kids are having trouble surviving in school post-COVID-19. I still think it was good advice to tell parents to not worry themselves with stress but to do the best they can. Kids are pretty resilient, but it is up to us as educators to step it up so they can achieve grade level competency. Hind-sight is 2020 indeed and now we know that most kids should have stayed in school. Of course, teachers worried about their health as well. No matter what choice was made back then, there were pros and cons for each.

The first edition of this book began the Introduction with this:

> This book begins with a sad reminder of how inspirational priorities can become sidetracked by politics and ideology. A couple of years ago, the last space shuttle was rocketed into space for the last time. From the NASA website:

> Space shuttle Atlantis lifted off from Launch Pad 39A at NASA's Kennedy Space Center in Florida at 11:29 a.m. EDT, July 8, 2011 on the STS-135 mission and final flight of the space shuttle program. Atlantis' final flight will cap off an amazing 30-year program of exploration, which launched great observatories, built an international space station, and taught us how humans can live, work and thrive in space. (Deiss, 2023, para. 4)

So ends the quest to return humans to the moon by 2020 (the project Constellation). In 2010, President Obama called for NASA to end its moon program, thereby cancelling the next generation of space shuttles (Malik, 2010). The administration suggests that the future of space exploration would be better served as a capitalistic private enterprise, with NASA buying tickets for its future astronauts to ride in aircraft built by others instead of NASA. Obama claims that ending the shuttle program would free up financial and human capital that would in turn, be funneled into new technologies and that space exploration would become an international endeavor; less tied to America's identity, and more to collaboration.

Unfortunately, in the current age of expanding wars and international financial collapse, it seems that space and exploration now take a backseat to more "practical" American concerns. This is counterproductive not only for America but for the world. Would a private sector space program truly have pure science at heart, or the interests of those funding the project? Should space exploration be a for-profit enterprise? Think about it; exploration is all about risk. With the government behind you, scientists are free to risk and experiment in the name of science. Private enterprise puts pressure on product and outcomes, and can be severely limiting to scientists who need to take risks. What private investor wants to risk his or her investment and money? How can this be good for science? And what does it say about a country that would rather finance multiple simultaneous wars than space exploration? Wars are fundamentally about our differences. Science, space exploration, and discovery are reminders of how we are all so very much the same.

Neil deGrasse Tyson, the director of the Hayden Planetarium and research associate in the department of astrophysics at the American Museum of Natural History and star of NOVA Science Now, has a lot to say about this topic. David Greene of National Public Radio (NPR) recently interviewed Dr. de Grasse-Tyson about the future of space exploration. de Grasse-Tyson (2013) explained:

> Space exploration is a force of nature unto itself that no other force in society can rival. Not only does that get people interested in sciences and all the related fields, [but] it transforms the culture into one that values science and technology, and *that's* the culture that innovates...What [the president] needs to say is, "We need to double NASA's budget because not only is it the grandest epic adventure a human being can undertake, not only would the people who led this

adventure be the ones we end up building statues to and naming high schools after and becoming the next generation's Mercury 7 as role models, not only will there be spinoff products from these discoveries, but what's more important than all of those, what's more practical than all of those, is that he will transform the economy into one that will lead the world once again rather than trail the world as we are inevitably going to be doing over the next decade." (As told to David Greene, February 27, 2012, "Space Chronicles: why Exploration Still Matters")

While we have no choice but to give President Obama the benefit of the doubt, there is much to lose if he is wrong. We do want collaboration between nations, we do want to go further than the moon one day, and we do want new technologies that could enable us to reach these destinations. Questions and repercussions concerning the privatization of the space program will have to be dealt with eventually. Maybe the future of space exploration is not dead, maybe it is going through a rebirth process. The fate of the future of scientific space discovery rests on the outcome. (Berube, pp. ix, x)

Preface

A little over 10 years ago I started the preface to the first edition of *STEM and the City* telling readers of my middle school science teaching experience in an urban public school. I also taught in a private school as well, but the urban middle school—in Norfolk, Virginia—ignited a passion in me for educating underserved children. This led to me pursuing a PhD in urban studies and urban education at Old Dominion University. Learning about poverty, inequality, and educational injustice formed me into the teacher educator I am today. With this edition, I am enlisting the help of a colleague and friend from high school, Dr. Sueanne McKinney. Sue taught middle school math in an urban school in Norfolk, Virginia. Sueanne also attended the same PhD program as me in urban studies and urban education at ODU. Over the years we have been a dynamic duo—writing articles and books on urban children and how best to meet their educational needs. It is a calling that has been full of purpose and meaning.

Then COVID-19 came along in 2020. Not only did the COVID-19 pandemic turn American education on its head, it set millions of students in a backwards direction in terms of development and learning—and those students are still suffering from this gap today. Students who were in kindergarten, first, and second grades who were learning how to read in 2020 are now struggling with literacy as they enter middle elementary school with millions of them far behind where they should be. And as for college students—those who were in high school when American schools shut down—they are now finding themselves in college having never written a term paper or learned how to conduct scholarly research. Teachers and professors everywhere are playing catch up with bright young people who, through no fault of their own, have found themselves struggling. Although I highly supported the efforts of America's medical leadership of the time who were just trying to do the best and least harmful thing for school children, the data did not lead to the assumption that schools should have been shut down. Nonetheless, schools across the nation were shut down, leaving confused and working parents to scramble as they adjusted and tried to "homeschool" their kids the best they could, which parenthetically made many parents realize how hard teaching truly is. The educational and socioemotional consequences have led to the current state where millions of school children are still trying to catch up academically, and it has led to more depression and anxiety that they have to deal with on top of playing catch up. This second edition of *STEM and the City* aims to address some issues caused by the pandemic, and to also bring to the forefront the importance of educating children who were underserved before the pandemic, and who are hanging on by a thread now. The workforce still needs STEM workers, but what does that look like after COVID-19? What happened to science classes during the pandemic? How can we not only get back to where we were but finally realize the great American dream? The United States has a gem in the American public school system, the greatest vehicle for democracy the world has ever known. Our kids deserve our best effort.

1

The History of STEM in American Public Schools

There was no such thing as STEM education when American public schools were conceived as an idea for fostering democracy and nation building. For starters, engineering would not be considered until George Washington realized its national importance, and technology had not yet exploded as a result of the industrial revolution in the 19th century. Science and mathematics were not seen as uniting concepts, but rather as separate, individual disciplines in the first American public schools. The idea that science and mathematics could be taught in relation to each other was centuries in the future, and certainly not on the minds of early settlers to the New World.

STEM as an acronym is fairly new; probably attributed to Vernon Ehlers, a congressman from Michigan; and is used to depict science, technology, engineering, and mathematics as fields that, while separate, are also interdependent and related. Ehlers was a professor of nuclear physics at the University of California at Berkeley before heading into political life, and as a congressman was asked by Newt Gingrich to coordinate science and education policy. The year was 1998 and policy had not been rewritten since 1945. Ehlers (2010) states:

> I should note that, over the years, the business and education community collectively referred to science, mathematics, engineering, and technology education as "SMET," and I introduced legislation referencing SMET. More recently, the community decided a more pleasant acronym was needed and referred to science, technology, engineering, and mathematics as STEM instead. (para. 7)

Various STEM fields can include chemistry, psychology and other social sciences, medicine, geosciences, biology and life sciences, astronomy and space sciences, oceanography and environmental sciences, engineering, computer science, and science education and technical training. The concept of STEM would take centuries to realize.

The great American experiment known as democratic public education began with the arrival of the Mayflower and the settlement of Plymouth colony in southeastern Massachusetts in 1620 by a group of Puritans from Plymouth England. A very religious group, they were nonetheless unhappy with the control the Anglican Church exercised over their affairs, and so sought separation of church and state. The vast majority of these settlers were literate and wanted to ensure that their children would be too, so education was on the top of their agenda as they settled into their new surroundings.

Coming as they were from urban England, these settlers were not educated in the ways of agriculture. Jamestown, Virginia was settled in 1607 by British settlers (American Journeys, n.d., AJ-073, p. 15), followed by another group of Pilgrim Puritans in 1620, who landed on Plymouth Rock in Massachusetts (American Journeys, n.d., AJ-025, p. 106). It was in their best interests to cooperate with Native Americans, who traded goods with the settlers in return for teaching them about the land. In the new colonies up and down the eastern seaboard, partnerships amongst the settlers and Native Americans thrived for a few years until the Powhatan Indians in Virginia got fed up with being used for food while being systematically pushed out of their own land. They revolted against the English settlers in 1622 as a result (American Journeys, n.d., AJ-082, p. 358), leaving the city dwellers to go it alone on the land. In the meantime, the science of agriculture learned in large part from the Native Americans, enabled early American settlers to live off the land up until and during the time of the great Westward expansion in the late 19th century. The schools of this time were concerned with moral training in order to overcome man's inherently evil natures as was the belief. Childhood depravity and uncontrolled speech was the natural state of man, and education, using the bible as the text, would purify society and turn people from sin. Science was mainly a practical matter in order to cultivate fields and build homes.

Universities took the lead. It took nothing less than warfare to get early American institutions of higher education interested in formalized science education. The United States Military Academy at West Point had been the most important military training institution in America since George Washington had overseen the building of the fortifications of the campus in 1778, enabling Washington to transfer his headquarters to West Point in 1779. From this perch atop a hill overlooking the Hudson River, Washington, along with other administrators including Alexander Hamilton and John Adams...all tired of America's dependence on foreign engineers...led an effort to create an institution of learning for the science of war at West Point, with civil engineering being the focus of the entire curriculum. Indeed, for the first half of the 19th century, West Point grads were responsible for the construction of most of the nation's bridges, railways, harbors, and roads (https://www.westpoint.edu/about/history-of-west-point/brief-history-of-west-point).

George Washington was considered America's first engineer. According to Boule II (2003):

> As a young man, Washington learned to survey. He had a natural talent for mathematics. At the age of 16, he apprenticed with several accomplished surveyors on a month-long trip to the Blue Ridge Mountains to survey Lord Fairfax's lands. He mastered the trade quickly, earning an appointment as county surveyor of Culpeper County, Virginia, at the age of 17. Washington later used his knowledge of topography and mapmaking to produce drawings of the Ohio River Valley in 1753, while on a dangerous mission to deliver a message to the French demanding their withdrawal from the region. These sketches represented the state of geographical knowledge of the area at the outbreak of the French and Indian War that occurred shortly after his trip. Even though he was heavily burdened as a Virginia planter, businessman, and legislator; commander of the Continental Army for eight years; and President of the United States for eight years, he is credited with conducting an extensive number of surveys. During his lifetime, Washington surveyed more than 200 tracts of land consisting of 60,000-plus acres. He is credited with drawing more than 100 maps, including a map of the city of Alexandria. He was involved with L'Enfant in planning the technical layout for the future capital city that would bear his name. (Boule II, 2003, para. 8–10)

Elsewhere in the country during the early to mid 1800s, the consensus for elementary curricula still seemed to be for a liberal education with the classics at its core. The "1828 Report by Faculty Committee," consisting of Yale faculty at the urging of Yale's president and fellows in response to a movement for a more progressive curriculum, came out with a defense of the classical curriculum, heavy on Latin and Greek literature. It should be mentioned here that even at West Point the scientific premise was for practical country building via engineering, less so for the more natural sciences.

The natural world was still met with some suspicion that those who wished to study it were ungodly and atheistic (ironically, that point is still being argued by some today). Natural science was considered "feminine" at a time when women were thought to be less human than men. Anyone who was considered connected to nature was thought to be more animalistic; even savage-like than those who were not. Since women took babies to the breast, this was evidence that women were less evolved than men. Even so, notable naturalists changed natural science forever. In the mid 18th century, Swedish botanist Carolus Linnaeus (the father of modern taxonomy) was busy figuring out classes of animals and plants and creating the natural taxonomy system still in use today. His basis for this taxonomy? The male prototype. Scientists of the time thought of the perfection of the male gender as the natural prototype to which all other living things are measured. Not only male, but White and European. When it came time to categorize animals and plants into a taxonomy, this prototype (maybe subconsciously) was the measuring stick. Just as in the Adam and Eve story, the male is considered the perfection of the species, and the woman a sub-type or defective version of the perfect male being.

Natural and biological science has historically been "women's" domain. According to Schiebinger (1993),

> Linnaeus thus followed well-established Western conceptions when he suggested that women belong to nature in ways that men do not. As Carolyn Merchant has shown, nature itself has long been conceived as female in most Western intellectual traditions. For the seventeenth century alchemist Michael Maier, the earth was literally a nourishing mother. (p. 56)

This has been called "the sexing of science." By the time early settlers were on America's shores, the influence of this mindset was foremost, and the work of the early schools was to train boys (not girls) out of their natural savage state, into a more intellectual, noble one. Women were considered more "of the earth"; more savage and primitive. The gendering (sexing) of biology and natural sciences (women's science); and physics, astronomy, and engineering (men's science) was born.

An exception was Darwin. British naturalist Charles Darwin was not yet a household name in the 1830s as he was presently undergoing surveying expeditions on the HMS Beagle; later becoming the poster boy for anti-science arguments made by the religious literal interpreters of the Bible. Along with Darwin, there were creative people, not necessarily scientists, who were persuasively writing about science and its benefits for human culture. Among them were Herbert Spencer and Edward Livingston Youmans. Spencer (1820–1903) was an English Victorian who wrote about philosophy, biology, and sociology. It was Spencer who coined "survival of the fittest" after reading Darwin's *On the Origin of the Species*, and who was widely read and popular (Weinstein, 2008). The topic of evolution has always been at the center of educational controversy. The Scopes trial (1925) will be discussed again in Chapter 2, but it did serve as the cornerstone of science education in American public schools in the early 20th century, effectively outlawing the teaching of evolution in public schools.

The British were the first to have a bona fide science teacher at the elementary level. William Sharp taught at a British public school called the Rugby School during the mid 1800s, and it was he who was credited with introducing science as a subject in the curriculum. Sharp developed a model for science education that was adopted throughout Britain (Leary, 2005). Science was about to become accessible to the general public, after many centuries of "ownership" by wealthy home-tutored private citizens in Europe and now in America.

Science in American Schools

Before the standardization of science in American public schools in the 1890s, the topic of science was mostly a hit or miss proposition, depending on the preferences of whoever was teaching it. Much of the scientific work of discovery and innovation had been done in other countries such as England and Switzerland and was dribbling into America as her immigrants landed on her eastern shores. Science teachers as such were newly in existence in England but not yet in America as of the progressive era of early 20th century. The concept of scientific education did not get formal recognition until July 1892, when the National Educational Association met for their conference in Saratoga New York to present their recommendations for admission to college. The National Education Association (NEA) appointed the "Committee of Ten" and charged them with coming up with recommendations on the subject of "uniformity in school programmes [sic] (standardization of the curriculum) and requirements for admission to college" (NEA, 1894, p. 3). The committee decided that the conference should convene meetings to decide about three areas of science: physics, astronomy, and chemistry; natural history; and geography. (Although not a Committee of Ten member, among the History, Government, and Political Economy conference was Woodrow Wilson, then a professor at the College of New Jersey. Other members included university faculty members and presidents, and head masters.) According to the Committee of Ten, the goal of education was to prepare most Americans for good citizenship, and some for college. The committee adopted a "citizen science approach" and said that elementary science should be based on observation of the natural world, while secondary science should focus on laboratory work and experiments; facts and principles should be taught, and that this should prepare students for college if they so desire. The committee suggested standardizing 12 years of schooling; 8 years of elementary and 4 years of high school and laid the groundwork for biology, chemistry, and physics during high school years. Natural science should be taught no less than twice weekly during elementary school (Mitchell, 1981). It took a while for these ideas to take hold.

Back in England in the meantime, the "Taunton Commission" was established to study the education of middle-class British boys. The commission decided to study girls also at the last minute. From 1864 to 1868 inspectors for the commission traveled throughout England—observing classes and interviewing teachers, headmasters, and other personnel. What they discovered was shocking; while science was barely being taught to boys, it was quite popular with girls in all-girl's schools. "While a boy's education was centered around Latin and Greek (thought to be more important), a girl's education included ample doses of botany, chemistry, natural philosophy, natural history and physiology" (Tolley, 1996, p. 129). Tolley (1996) also states that similar conditions were apparent in America during the same time frame. "The data supports the thesis that by 1840, the subjects of natural philosophy, chemistry, and astronomy had become more prevalent in American schools for middle and upper-class girls than in comparable institutions for boys (p. 129). This supported the mindset of the time that women needed to be "engineers" of their households and needed to be educated in science in order to run a proper home. According to Tolley's article, "Science for Ladies, Classics for Gentlemen: A Comparative Analysis of Scientific Subjects in the Curricula of Boys' and Girls' Secondary Schools in the United States, 1794–1850" (p. 131), the rationale for educating young women was to prepare them for their roles as mothers, wives, and teachers—not for leadership positions in society. Women "must be able to comprehend (her husband's) plans; she must sympathize in his feelings, or else she cannot be his helpmate" (p. 131). Secondary American science education for young women was aimed at producing well-informed wives capable of helping someone else (her husband) achieve their ambitions.

Emergence of Science as a Separate Subject

Elementary science had not yet been implemented as a subject in late 19th century America, and there certainly were no science textbooks as of yet. "Readers" were the books of choice in many subjects; teaching children how to read especially. Any science that elementary students were exposed to happened by chance as a result of these "readers" that were teaching children history or reading skills. Readers and textbooks, in general, were popular because most public-school teachers were poorly trained and needed the textbooks in order to teach appropriately. According to Rillero (2010),

> Reading was the most important subject, and readers were the most important textbooks... The focus was on reading, writing, and arithmetic. There were no science textbooks, and science was not taught as a separate subject (Underhill, 1941). Students learned about science through content area selections in the readers. Thus, the science in readers was the origin of American elementary science education. The science lessons in the readers of the first few years of school were students' first exposure to school science. Most students did not attend school past the first several years. Prior to 1890, only 3.8% of the population between 14 and 17 years of age enrolled in school (Hurd, 1961). Thus, for many 19th-century American school children, the science selections in the primary readers may have been the only formal science education encountered. The science in these readers was for all students the first school science experience, for many it was the only science experience, and from a historical perspective it was the cradle of American science education. (p. 278)

Rillero (2010) conducted a study to examine the role of early "readers" in science education. The decline of science in the readers over the years, correlated with the emergence of science as a separate subject. Rillero states,

> In the mid-19th century, science was firmly embedded in the first "R" of the three "Rs" of education, and students received significant science education in their reading. As science was pushed out of readers it began gaining credibility as a stand-alone subject. Science education was free to evolve into more than just something to read about, and it could grow as a subject for children to directly examine in the living world and non-living materials. Yet it has never shaken its roots as a subject in a textbook. Unfortunately, as science was pushed out of readers, it was also pushed out of the day-

to-day school experiences of many primary grade children. And it has not returned. (p. 283)

Engineering and Technology for Everyone

By the latter half of the 20th century, the focus had turned back to science education, due in part to the Soviet launch of the satellite Sputnik on October 14, 1957 and the start of the "space race" between America and Russia. The launch of Sputnik was directly responsible for the creation of NASA in July 1958, when Congress passed the National Aeronautics and Space Act, which sparked an interest in STEM subjects across America (Anonymous, 2013). According to Yager (2000),

> In the late 1950s, Soviet space exploits resulted in massive reforms—a new game—in U.S. school science that were drastically different from past reforms. The reforms of the late 1950s and 1960s were led by scientists whose aim was to change the game so that all learners would experience and know the science that scientists know and practice the skills that scientists use to understand the objects and events that make up the natural universe. Scientists in the various disciplines sought to produce visions of the big ideas of their disciplines that could provide the frameworks for new courses in schools. (p. 51)

Indeed, the idea of sending a man to the moon during that time was intoxicating, and spurred on a generation of children with dreams of becoming astronauts and scientists. It is interesting to note, however, that in sharp contrast to the current model of STEM education as integrating science, technology, engineering, and mathematics, the model that resulted from the space race purposefully omitted these other content areas:

> Leaders in school science also attempted to rid the curriculum of the subject of technology (e.g., television, transportation, communication, home appliances). Textbooks and science teachers ceased to refer to technical careers, a topic that then incorporated into vocational programs for the non-college bound student. (p. 51)

The irony of the short-sightedness of this mindset was to become apparent 30 years later as the Silicon Valley produced brilliant minds who would lead the entire world in a technology revolution, far away from the college classroom.

As was noted earlier, George Washington was America's first engineer, sparking the induction of the U.S. Army Engineer School. Early engineering was seen as a subject only future engineers would take in order to train them for their careers. Technology education in primary and secondary public schools is seen as the stepping stone for more formal engineering. vo-tech (vocational-technical) schools have been in existence for many years in America, as specialized high schools or programs in high schools that train students in careers requiring certain skills not found in college—such as electrician, plumbing, and mechanical. There are very prestigious colleges and universities that can be technically considered vocational or trade schools—or at the very least have components of such programs—such as Massachusetts Institute of Technology (MIT) and California Institute of Technology (Caltech). However, most vo-tech schools graduate students in the trade fields. At the primary level, engineering and technology are not taught as separate subjects, but elements of both may be incorporated into either the mathematics or science curriculum.

Chapter 7 will propose to show what effective modern day science teaching looks like. It has changed in many ways since the 1970s, when much of science was taught in lecture format like any other subject—albeit with a test tube and beaker thrown in for good measure. The changes we see in science classrooms—both elementary and secondary—can still be attributed to the space race in the late 1950s and to later educational movements—such as the standards and testing movements. Some of these changes are for the worse; some are true evolutions in methodology that raise the level of understanding. Chapter 6 will discuss the effects that No Child Left Behind and Race to the Top have had on science and STEM education. One of the major problems that developed has been the temptation to "teach to the test"; reducing science to multiple choice answers on a bubble test, and the dumbing down of science in order to pass these high-stakes state mandated tests. We have come a long way but we still have so far to go—especially in these times of heightened anti-intellectualism and disdain of science. Arguably, science teachers hold the future of America in their hands.

2

American Anti-Intellectualism, Religion, and the Science Classroom

Culture War of the Worlds

On June 19, 2024, Louisiana Governor Jim Landry signed House Bill 71 into law, which made it a requirement for every classroom that receives state funding (public schools) from kindergarten to university, to post an easily readable version of the Ten Commandments. No doubt the ACLU and other civil liberties groups will sue the governor, citing that this law undermines the separation of church and state. According to Gallman and Gallagher (2024):

> Opponents of the bill have argued that a state requiring a religious text in all classrooms would violate the establishment clause of the U.S. Constitution, which says that congress can "make no law respecting an establishment of religion." Civil liberties groups swiftly vowed to challenge the law—which makes Louisiana the first in the nation to require the Ten Commandments be displayed in every classroom that receives state funding—in court. The American Civil Liberties Union, the American Civil Liberties Union of Loui-

siana, Americans United for Separation of Church and State, and the Freedom From Religion Foundation said that the law violates the long-standing Supreme Court precedent and the First Amendment and would result in "unconstitutional religious coercion of students." "The First Amendment promises that we all get to decide for ourselves what religious beliefs, if any, to hold and practice, without pressure from the government. Politicians have no business imposing their preferred religious doctrine on students and families in public schools," the groups said in a joint statement. (paras. 6–9)

The founding of America was based in large part on the resistance of its citizens to be held to any one religious doctrine—freedom of, and from religion. The founding fathers thought this so important that they included it in the constitution. Those who signed the Declaration of Independence were progressive intellectuals, who had the foresight to try to protect future Americans from the dogma and oppression that they and their ancestors had recently suffered in England. Now we are faced with a curious problem; some in powerful political positions seek to turn America *into* a religiously led country, even going so far as to say that only those who follow their narrow Christian views are the only true Americans. What is the effect of this mentality on scientific exploration and progress in modern American culture?

Anti-Intellectualism and American Society

In modern America, school districts across America are ripping pages out of text books that teach American history pertaining to slavery—banning books the right-wing Christian movement doesn't agree with and omitting any content deemed progressive or dare I say... true? Florida has been the worst offender so far. In 2023, Republican Governor Ron DaSantis made it his priority to turn back the clock in schools by decades, putting Florida children behind the curve in learning and content. According to Roberts (2023):

> Ron DeSantis got a good education at Dunedin High School (under Democratic Gov. Lawton Chiles, I might add), Yale College, and Harvard Law. He had the chance to encounter a variety of ideas: No one forced him to agree. He was allowed to read a variety of texts, about which he could form his own judgments. He was free to learn. Today, the students of Florida are not. Bent on keeping children as ignorant as possible, local school authorities, egged on by those neo-Puritans calling themselves "Moms for Liberty," are banning books that might suggest that gay and lesbian and trans kids are actual human beings. This is not just "Don't Say Gay," it's don't be gay. Don't be yourself. Be who Ron DeSantis tells you to be. Kids were supposed to have a lesson on Michelangelo's statue of David and Botticelli's "Birth of Venus," scandalously bra-less as she floats in from the sea. David is naked as a jaybird

and sports his junk for all the world to see. The parental freak-out brigade did not see beauty or a celebration of the human form. One of them called it pornography. (paras. 1–12)

It feels like we are back in time. In 1963 Richard Hofstadter, a progressive professor of history at Columbia University and public intellectual, wrote a seminal book on American culture entitled *Anti-Intellectualism in American Life*. The book went on to win the 1964 Pulitzer Prize for nonfiction. Hofstadter describes America's fear of intellectualism and cities in general. He blames xenophobic ideas and anti-Semitism for this fear of cities, and said that it came to a head during the McCarthy era. Hofstadter also mentions that America has become provincial and backwards compared to its European counterparts. Hofstadter notes that during the 1950s, at the height of McCarthyism, American Ivy League universities came under scrutiny as being hotbeds of Communism. Indeed, colleges and universities in general were seen by the right-wing as training grounds for the liberal agenda. Hofstadter presents several "exhibits" from the literature of the day to make his point that anti-intellectualism was rife in American society:

> Universities, particularly the better-known universities, were constantly marked-out by right wing critics; but according to one writer in the *Freeman*, there appears to have been only an arbitrary reason for this discrimination against the Ivy League, since he considered that Communism is spreading in all our colleges: "Our universities are the training grounds for the barbarians of the future; those who, in the guise of learning, shall come forth loaded with pitchforks of ignorance and cynicism, and stab and destroy the remnants of human civilization. It will not be the subway peasants who will tear down the walls; they will merely do the bidding of our learned brethren... who will erase individual freedom from the ledgers of human thought." (p. 13)
>
> If you send your son to the colleges of today, you will create the executioner of tomorrow. The rebirth of idealism must come from the scattered monasteries of non-collegiate thought. (p. 14)

Those on the religious right are in many cases leading the charge against intellectualism in America today. Especially targeted are still American colleges and universities. During the 2012 presidential election cycle, we saw the Republican presidential candidate Rick Santorum, a conservative Catholic, bash college and university education, even as he holds three college degrees, including a JD—which is a form of a doctorate—from Penn State University. During the race to the primaries, Santorum called President Obama a "snob" because of his elite education. According to *The Washington Post*:

> Rick Santorum calls it snobbery to suggest that students ought to go to college. On Monday, several of his fellow Republicans—and President Obama—begged to differ. Some GOP governors in Washington for the National Governors Association took issue with Santorum's remark, which he made Saturday as he mounted a last-minute sprint for votes before Tuesday's primary in Michigan. "I wish he'd said it differently," Virginia Gov. Robert F. McDonnell said of Santorum. "When you look at what's going on in other countries—China, India, the premium they put on higher education—we've got to do better if we still want to be the global leader we are." (Somashekhar & Nakamura, 2012, para. 3)

This smokescreen pervades the Republican party at all levels. President Trump's new head of the Pentagon, Pete Hegseth, who got a master's degree in public policy at Harvard University, actually sent his diploma back to the school and said on live television that he is dumber because of going to Harvard. Anyone with that much privilege who can spit in the face of an elite school, should be ashamed. Trump's Republican party does not value education. The disingenuousness of the right on this issue is highly disturbing, especially since their platform is economic growth.

Trump's latest (as of early summer 2025) war with Harvard is in full swing. Recently President Trump threatened to cancel hundreds of millions of dollars of grants and contracts if Harvard continues to register foreign students. On June 5, 2025, a judge blocked Trump's ban on Harvard's foreign students from entering the United States (*The Guardian*, June 5, 2025). The Trump administration is not interested in what is best for the American people, the economy, or for the general welfare of Americans. His administration is interested in power, money for themselves, and pushing the clock back to a time when only White males ruled the world. They see an educated population as a huge threat. They should know: they have that education.

The brain-washing of the American public against its own interests is not new. During the Nixon administration, the "Southern strategy" was employed in order to win Southern White democratic votes. Many younger people today cannot picture a South that is mostly Democratic, but such was the case. Nixon discouraged his fellow Republicans from blocking the Black vote, because in his mind with more Blacks voting, Southern Whites would abandon the Democratic Party for the Republican Party, and that's just what happened. Many times in our nations' history, seemingly natural courses of events were actually carefully crafted behind-the-scenes strategies plotted out and conducted in order to achieve a political agenda— mostly without the knowledge of the American people. The Southern strategy was one, anti-intellectualism is another. If enough Americans turn their backs on science, then corporations can claim to be doing "God's work" with the environment, all the while maximizing profits to record levels. We must never forget that an uneducated populace is one that is easily controlled and manipulated. Does it ever dawn on people that these very same leaders who denounce university education as the domain of the "intellectually snobby elite," are themselves highly educated? Does anyone ever wonder how on earth religion and God became the property of the anti-environmental movement? Certain things are correlated through no accident, but through purposeful and intentional strategy. These ideas then become part of the American landscape, and we think it's natural and innocent. As is the case with religion and science.

As a professor who teaches science to preservice teachers, I have run across certain difficulties from time to time in my science teaching. The problem stems from beliefs that some students have about religion that prevent them from accepting scientific explanations about phenomena. For example, evolution seems to ignite controversy because some students don't believe that the earth has been found to be 4.54 billion years old. According to the Bible, it is only about 6,000 years old. If your parent is a minister, or if you adhere to a strict Biblical interpretation of the world, then you may have a problem with science. I am not saying here that one shouldn't be allowed to live in a free country and to believe however they choose; I am saying that science demands objective scrutiny. This mindset can hold back scientific progress in America.

Literacy is crucial for the preservation of a democratic society. Scientific literacy (which will be mentioned in more depth in Chapter 6) is a vital part of literacy in general. According to *Science for All Americans* (American Association for the Advancement of Science, 1990),

> Without a science-literate population, the outlook for a better world is not promising. Most Americans are not science-literate. One only has to look at the international studies of educational performance to see that U.S. students rank near the bottom in science and mathematics—hardly what one would expect if the schools were doing their jobs well. (p. xv)

What is scientific literacy?

> Science literacy—which encompasses mathematics and technology as well as the natural and social sciences—has many facets. These include being familiar with the natural world and respecting its unity; being aware of some of the important ways in which mathematics, technology, and the sciences depend upon one another; understanding some of the key concepts and principles of science; having a capacity for scientific ways of thinking; know-

ing that science, mathematics, and technology are human enterprises, and knowing what that implies about their strengths and limitations; and being able to use scientific knowledge and ways of thinking for personal and social purposes. (pp. xvii, xviii)

and

knowledge of the way science works is the requisite for scientific literacy. (p. 1)

In 2009, I wrote a letter to The Chronicle of Higher Education expressing my frustration on this topic.

LEARNING ABOUT GOD FROM FOSSILS   MAY 25, 2009

To the Editor:

I have to respectfully disagree with Arri Eisen and David Westmoreland ("Teaching Science, With Faith in Mind," *The Chronicle*, May 1). A science professor's responsibility is to teach science in an objective way, which is the whole intent of the scientific method and is what separates science from other fields. We don't do our students any favors by watering down science.

This dichotomy is artificial in the first place, because one can believe in God and in science—in fact, some of the best scientists who ever lived did just that (Einstein being just one). Nevertheless, I've run across problems when I was teaching the big bang or evolution and some of my students disagreed with me because they were raised with different beliefs and were taught different things. Where believers run into problems is in the "what happened when" timeline. But science has math on its side, and we can pretty much say with surety how old a fossil is, for instance, because of technology like carbon dating. Who can argue with carbon dating? Instead of arguing that something happened at a certain time, why not just open up to the possibility that God might have created the world just this way, with evolution and big bangs and millions of years of fossils? I've never had a problem with looking at evolution and considering how clever whoever did this must be. In fact, I believe that science will tell us more about God than any book.

Science is thankfully not open to personal opinion, which makes it pure, like mathematics. To pull punches in the teaching of science does not move us forward.

Clair Berube
The Chronicle of Higher Education, May 25, 2009.

This conflict between science and religion is not new... going back to the Scopes vs. Tennessee trial in 1925, where a teacher was sued for teaching evolution to his class, thereby breaking the new law in Tennessee that stated the teaching of evolution to be unlawful because it went against the teachings of the Bible. The teacher was John T. Scopes, and his attorney was Clarence Darrow—the most famous defense attorney in the nation at the time. The prosecuting attorney was William Jennings Bryan, a celebrated religious leader. The trial garnered much publicity and dogmatic battles in the press. Judge John T. Raulston sided with the prosecution time and time again, even as Scopes and Darrow made intellectual mincemeat of Bryan. Scopes was found guilty, but the verdict was overturned by the State Supreme Court. The state however, upheld the anti-evolution law until 1967 when it was finally repealed (Bennen, 2000, pp. 60–63).

Armenta and Lane (2010) take this fight up to present day textbook adoption in Texas and to the stance courts have taken to uphold separation of church and state. Texas is a large purchaser of textbooks, and fights within the state government over the teaching of evolution have not gone away over the years. The Texas board of education has a huge influence over content in science textbooks. Armenta and Lane quote a story from MSNBC stating: "As one of the largest textbook purchasers in the nation, Texas has significant influence over the content of books marketed across the country" (Castro, 2009, p. 79). Armenta and Lane conclude, "By and large, courts consistently have ruled against efforts to endorse or promote religion. Likewise, they have frowned upon school districts and states that try to promote religion under the pretense of balanced treatment, academic freedom, or critical thinking" (Castro, 2009, p. 79). However, problems and struggles continue.

Race

The question becomes: "How does religious identification and literal interpretation of religious texts influence scientific literacy?" Darren Sherkat (2011; Southern Illinois University) has written an article entitled "Religion and Scientific Literacy in the United States" in which he examines how adherence to strict religious dogma affects scientific literacy. Independent variables included sectarian and Catholic identifications, no identifications, and the importance of fundamentalist versus secular beliefs about the Bible and other religious books, education, income, race, region, and gender. The dependent variable (scientific literacy) was measured using the 2006 General Social Survey ([GSS]; p. 1135). Sherkat cites research (Berkman et al., 2008; Darnell & Sherkat, 1997; Ellison & Musick, 1995;

Lienesch, 2007) that states, "Christian fundamentalist beliefs are rooted in the position that Christian sacred texts are inerrant, and should be taken as true representations of earth and human history" (p. 1136). As I mentioned earlier, literal interpretations of the Bible can affect how a person learns or doesn't learn science.

Sectarian Protestant denominations include the Southern Baptist Convention, Church of Christ, and Assembly of God. These groups have been at the forefront of opposition to teaching about evolution (Sherkat, 2011, p. 1137). What about race and religion? It should not go without noting that most African-Americans belong to religious groups. According to Sehgal and Smith (2009) with the Pew Forum on Religion and Public Life, Blacks are more religious on a variety of measures than the U.S. population as a whole. Seventy eight percent of African-Americans are Protestant (compared with 50% of the general population); 40% of these claiming to be Baptist, 5% Catholic, and less than half a percentage point are atheists.

> By several measures, including importance of religion in life, attendance at religious services and frequency of prayer, the historically Black Protestant group is among the most religiously observant traditions. In fact, on these and other measures of religious practices and beliefs, members of historically Black Protestant churches tend to resemble members of evangelical Protestant churches, another highly religious group. (Sehgal & Smith, 2009, para. 8).

What are the implications of this research? Studies show that STEM careers are the jobs of the future (Basso, 2012; Carnegie Science Center, 2012; Engler, 2012; Langdon et al., 2012; Locke, 2012). According to Locke (2012),

> In comparison to their non-STEM counterparts, STEM workers earn 26 percent more on average and are less likely to experience joblessness.
>
> Meanwhile, STEM degree holders enjoy higher earnings, regardless of their occupation. And no matter what their major, college graduates who work in a STEM job enjoy an earnings premium. (paras. 7–8)

Studies also show that African-Americans are underrepresented in STEM fields (Loftus, 2012; Palmer et al., 2010; Payton, 2004). In addition to the factors presented in Chapter 3 in the discussion of high-needs urban schools, could religiosity and belief systems be a determining factor in the low rates of African-Americans in STEM fields? It is vital that the brain-drain of African-Americans from STEM fields is halted, and it is very important that a possible contributing source of African-American underrepresentation in STEM is recognized and dealt with, no matter how politically incorrect or unpleasant. This holds for all groups whose religious beliefs stand in the way of scientific progress. The inability of much of America to reconcile religion or belief system with science is a problem not found in other industrialized countries. In order to maintain American competitiveness, we must be able to let the evidence lead the way. The jobs of the future demand it. We cannot afford to leave anyone behind.

In 2024, with Joe Biden as president, there was still a culture war raging about what should be taught in school. Donald Trump is president again, with his promise to ban books and squelch any history that teaches the truth about our American heritage. The state of Florida has created a curriculum that is almost unrecognizable in its re-writing of history. Believing that White children can't handle the truth about our history, it is simply erased. The teaching of slavery, when it appears at all, mutes the truth and states that slaves learned good skills as slaves that they used later. White nationalism, hiding under the cloak of Christianity, claims that all learning should be religion-based and they misread the founding fathers' purpose to limit the influence of religion on public life by saying that they meant everything to be Christian. The United States cannot allow itself to be dragged into the types of situations we have seen in the past—pro-autocracy systems of government where book burning and propaganda pass as education. Politicians with autocratic slants hate American public education because it offers a way for us to climb the ladder to the American dream. For a long time, and as the 2024 presidential election approached, Republicans doubled down on their claim that they would eliminate the Department of Education. In November of 2023 the House Republicans proposed a budget that drastically cut support for public education. Not only would the bill eliminate funding for disadvantaged students but would also cut funding for teacher and principal supports (Shoemaker-DeMio et al., 2023). As promised, after Trump regained the presidency, he enlisted the world's richest man, Elon Musk, to wield a chain saw to the government; slashing thousands of jobs and departments. The Department of Education was slashed up to 50% during the Spring of 2025. The political right sees education as a threat to the status-quo and there is a reason they are trying to cripple the great American vehicle for democracy—public education. Autocratic countries with dictators withhold high quality education from their people. Is the United States of America next?

3

The Pedagogy of Poverty vs. Real STEM Teaching in Urban, High Poverty Schools

The general public—and even educators alike—often misperceive the definition of an urban school, as well as how it fits into the Title I spectrum. Using an "urban-centric," methodological classification system, the National Center for Educational Statistics (2023), catalogue all schools into four locales. These locales include size, population density, and their relation to city/urban schools, which are typically in or near within a metropolitan area, and service students who are experiencing poverty or are poor and who are ethnically diverse, in densely populated areas. Many of these schools and students are often portrayed as lower achieving environments and individuals, with a sizable percentage of student mobility, and difficulty in attracting and retaining effective, qualified leadership and teachers. According to Haberman (1995, 2005), Hill-Jackson and Stafford (2017), and Kincheloe (2004), urban schools are viewed as environments where students demonstrate persistently low academic achievement, school instructional coherence is unbalanced, they contain a poorly prepared and inexperienced teaching faculty (often first year teachers who demonstrate low expectations and fixed mindsets), and an inadequately functioning bureaucracy.

Urban schools are classified based on a Title I spectrum, based on the number of students receiving free and reduced lunch prices. Bouchrika (2024) explains that President Lyndon B. Johnson's War on Poverty Policy Act in 1965 established the foundation of a Title I school. It has since shifted to the No Child Left Behind Act of 2001. The aim of the program is to give disadvantaged children an equal opportunity for academic success through additional, apportioned funding by the U.S. government (Bajak et al., 2020). Any school with a significant percentage of high-poverty students may participate in the program. The U.S. Department of Education (2024) affirms that Title I was developed to guarantee that underprivileged students obtain a just, yet high-quality education by bridging gaps in educational achievement and "racial and ethnic equality in student outcomes" (McNair et al., 2020, p. 103). Many consider this funding the largest federal assistance program for public school children.

A school district can use Title I school funding in a variety of ways that emphasize advancing and improving the academic success and goals of high-poverty students through academic opportunities, availability of counselors, increasing parental involvement and participation, increasing staff employment, to name a few. However, according to the U.S. Department of Education (2024), Title I funds are extensively used to increase reading and math scholarship.

Becky Pringle, president of the National Educational Association, states thatwhen Joe Biden was president, he was committed to impacting the lives of our most vulnerable population, and this occurred through the Title I fund (National Education Association, 2021). Table 3.1 shows the January 2022 Monthly Child Poverty Rates. The chart depicts the highest poverty rate since the end of 2020 due to the Child Tax Credit payments, which provided backbone to Biden's devotion to assisting those in most need of Title I funding.

Since President Trump took office, funding education has sharply decreased. According to Walker (2025), "On May 2, the Trump administration unveiled its blueprint for the fiscal year 2025–26 federal budget. Since it does not list specific funding requests for every federal program, the 46-page document is a "skinny" budget. Congress ultimately decides how federal government dollars are spent (the fiscal year begins October 1) but the proposal is a clear signal of the White House's priorities: a massive 23 percent cut to U.S. domestic spending, and, in the process, continue hollowing out the nation's public education system.

TABLE 3.1 January 2022 Monthly Child Poverty Rates by Children's Race and Ethnicity

	SPM Child Poverty Rate (%)			
Children	December 2021	January 2022	Percentage Pt. Change	Percent Change
All	12.1%	17.0%	4.9 p.p.	41.1%
White	7.5%	11.4%	3.9 p.p.	52.3%
Black	19.5%	25.4%	5.9 p.p.	30.4%
Latino	16.8%	23.9%	7.1 p.p.	42.5%
Asian	11.9%	15.1%	3.2 p.p	26.9%
	Number in Poverty			
Children	December 2021	January 2022	Increase	
All	8,912,000	12,574,000	3,662,000	
White	2,750,000	4,189,000	1,438,000	
Black	2,175,000	2,837,000	662,000	
Latino	3,165,000	4,509,000	1,344,000	
Asian	519,000	659,000	410,000	

Source: Parolin, Collyer, & Curran (2022), Center on Poverty and Social Policy at Columbia University, Monthly SPM Poverty for January 2022.

Note: Numbers rounded to the nearest thousand.

This should come as no surprise to anyone following the administration's actions over the past 100 days. Through a flurry of executive orders—including ordering the dismantling of the U.S. Department of Education—the administration has made gutting education funding, and diverting taxpayer dollars to private schools, a major priority of Trump's second term. No federal education program—almost none—has been spared.

The budget proposal would slice $12 billion from the Department of Education, eliminate many K–12 and higher education programs—reflecting funding levels of an agency, in the words of Education Secretary Linda McMahon, "that is responsibly winding down."

In fact, said NEA President Becky Pringle, the proposed cuts are a "slap in the face" to educators and students across the nation:

> For too long, parents, educators and students have pleaded with elected leaders to live up to their promise to every student and provide the resources give them every opportunity to thrive. And for too long, our leaders have failed us, and this is yet another example [...] Rather than investing in opportunity and equity, this proposal advances a harmful agenda that slashes essential programs millions of Americans rely on every day. (Walker, 2025, para. 1–5)

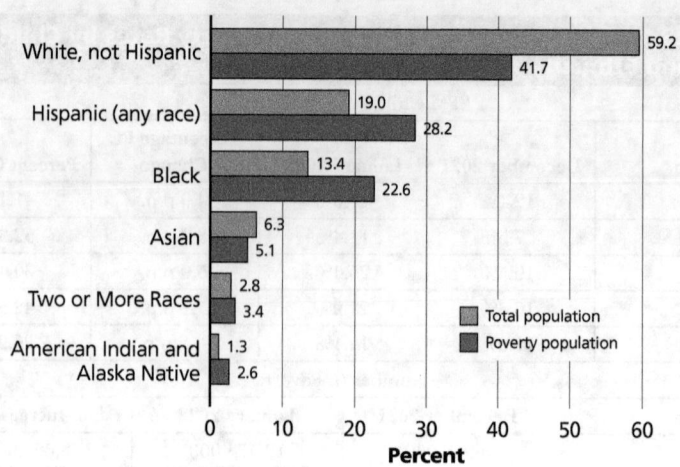

Figure 3.1 Distribution of total population and poverty by race using the official poverty measure: 2021. *Source:* Parolin et al. (2022).

According to the National Center for Educational Statistics (2023), in 2023, enrollment in public schools increased from 49.5% to 50.8% in 2022, dropping slightly during the coronavirus pandemic. However, many might find the change quite surprising. Parolin et al. (2022) reported a monthly increase in poverty rates in January 2022, pointing out this has been the highest increased rate since poverty attributable to the termination of the monthly Child Tax Credit payments. Latino and African American children experienced the largest increase (7.1 percentage points and 5.9 percentage points, respectively). Figure 3.1 projects the total population and poverty by race.

The Pedagogy of Poverty

All kinds of teaching methodologies can be found in urban classrooms. However, a typical style and form of teaching tends to dominate the classroom and has been accepted by educators and the community (Haberman, 2005). Since 1955, these acts of teaching have become more common and customary. Is it because the teacher's ideology is undergirded by the research that articulates that scholarship and test scores of the disadvantaged are affected by their socioeconomic class and ethnicity (Haberman, 2005)?

These acts of teaching are the evidence used today that define acceptable urban teaching and include the following:

- giving information
- giving directions
- making assignments

- reviewing assignments
- asking questions
- monitoring seatwork
- assigning homework
- reviewing homework
- punishing non-compliance
- settling disputes
- grading papers
- giving tests
- reviewing tests
- giving grades (Haberman, 2005, pp. 47–48)

These practices are not supported by research, or theory, and are a set of ritualistic acts to control students and their behavior instead of igniting a passion for life-long learning (Haberman, 2005). So why are they so readily accepted in urban schools and communities? Haberman states that many parents were not successful in school themselves and have not had great models of exceptional teachers. Many teachers lack the ability to participate in personal reflection and thoughtful analysis and may fear minorities and impoverished children. Low expectations for minorities and limited instructional practices and strategies also contribute to the pedagogy of poverty practices (Haberman, 1991).

Exceptional STEM Teachers or "Stars"

Science, technology, engineering, and mathematics (STEM) opportunities, experiences, and initiatives should be offered and provided to *all* students regardless of race, ethnicity, language or culture, ability, income level, or gender (Capraro & Slough, 2009). Because of the coronavirus pandemic's devastating effect on children, Mervosh (2022) stated that it "erased nearly two decades of progress in math and reading" (para. 1). This was seen mostly in 9-year-old students from racial minority groups—in other words, those who are the most disadvantaged and vulnerable (Mervosh, 2022).

While STEM concentration is moving forward globally, the emphasis continues to elude many schools nationwide, especially those that are underprivileged and with a high concentration of students in poverty. While living in impoverished areas alone doesn't determine their success in school and their adeptness and talent to pursue STEM careers, the literature suggests that there is a direct relationship between poverty and the likelihood that students housed in these schools will be provided with the necessary resources and effective teachers needed to facilitate a rich, stimulating STEM learning environment (National Research Council, 2011).

The critical demand of high-quality teachers and instruction for high-poverty schools is of particular concern for educators and students alike nationwide. Dating back for decades, the research evidence validates a distinct correlation between student academic achievement and the quality of the education (Carter & Welner, 2013; Haberman, 1995, 2005; Haberman et al., 2018; Hill-Jackson & Stafford, 2017; Hill-Jackson et al., 2019). However, the educational community continues to participate in spirited debates on the qualities, characteristics, and dispositions that define an effective teacher. Although the No Child Left Behind Act of 2002 established criteria—such as test scores and pedigrees for defining high-quality teachers—the achievement gap racial disparities and inequities continue to dominate these schools and populations (Hill-Jackson et al., 2019; Perie et al., 2005). Vital qualitative characteristics and teacher dispositions are nowhere mentioned in defining a high-quality teacher according to the NCLB Act (2002), yet these are the attributes imperative to urban student success (McKinney et al., 2006)

Urban students critically need an effective teacher since the United States is experiencing an increasing presence of minority populations, for example, African Americans and Latinos (Clewell et al., 2007; Hill-Jackson & Stafford, 2017). Undoubtedly, "the nation will become more dependent on their contributions to maintain its ascendancy in the global economy" (Clewell & Campbell, 2007, p. 3).

A teacher's ideology in assisting students during STEM project-based activities is especially momentous. These teachers must have the skills, knowledge, and dispositions to actualize STEM activities by enforcing fifteen functions identified by Haberman (1995, 2005). According to Haberman (1995), those such teachers who can put into practice these functions during STEM instruction—or for that matter any content instruction or classroom management—are able to recognize the potential and individual giftedness and talents within all students.

Haberman (1995) endeared the term "Star Teachers" to capture the essence of these exceptional educators. As described by Haberman (1995, 2005), Star Teachers are

> teachers who, by all common criteria, are outstandingly successful: their students score higher on standardized tests; parents and children think they are great; principals rate them highly; other teachers regard them as outstanding; central office supervisors consider them successful; cooperating universities regard them as superior; and they evaluate themselves as outstanding teachers. (1995, p. 1)

Table 3.2 summarizes the identified functions.

TABLE 3.2 Star Teachers' Functions as Identified by Haberman

Characteristic	Description
Protecting Children's Learning	Teachers can capitalize on all learning opportunities.
Persistence	Teachers constantly pursue strategies and activities so that all students can meet success.
Approach to At-Risk Students	Teachers take responsibility for children's learning, regardless of the conditions they face.
Putting Ideas Into Practice	Teachers can relate theory and practice.
Professional/Personal Orientation to Students	Teachers expect and can develop rapport with children.
The Bureaucracy	Teachers can adjust and cope with the demands of the bureaucracy.
Fallibility	Teachers take responsibility for their own errors and mistakes.
Emotional and Physical Stamina	Teachers can endure the challenges and crises of urban settings.
Organizational Ability	Teachers have extraordinary organizational and managerial skills.
Explanation of Teacher Success	Teachers believe that success is met by effort and hard work and not by ability alone.
Explanation of Student Success	Teachers are committed to student autonomy and individual differences.
Real Teaching	Teachers engage in active teaching instead of direct instruction.
Making Students Feel Needed	Teachers can make the students feel needed and wanted in the classroom.
Gentle Teaching in a Violent Society	Teacher's ideology is promising, even considering a violent society.
The Material vs. the Student	Teachers find approaches that will assist students in mastering the material.

Source: Haberman (1995)

For over 40 years, other independent scholars also investigated the characteristics and dispositions needed to be effective with children facing poverty. There is a distinct correspondence between all research teams, as you can see in Table 3.3. Taken together, or viewed as independent functions of Star Teachers, all hold the promise of offering culturally driven and equity inclusive STEM instruction. Especially noteworthy is Haberman's (1995, 2005) argument that a teacher's approach to working with at-risk students is the most powerful indicator of their success with urban learners. He states:

> At-risk students are the most powerful predictor. There is no question that those predisposed to blame the victim will fail as teachers, while those whose

TABLE 3.3 Individual Scholar's Research on the Characteristics Needed for Effective Urban Teaching

Haberman (1995, 2005)	Campbell et al. (1983)	Baron et al. (1992)	Abbate-Vaughn et al. (2010)	Poplin et al. (2011)	Robinson & Lewis (2017)
Protecting Children's Learning	X	X		X	
Persistence					
Approach to At-Risk Students			X	X	X
Putting Ideas Into Practice		X	X		
Professional/Personal Orientation to Students	X		X	X	
The Bureaucracy					
Fallibility					
Emotional and Physical Stamina					
Organizational Ability		X			
Explanation of Student Success			X	X	
Explanation of Teacher Success			X		
Real Teaching	X	X	X	X	
Making Students Feel Needed	X		X		X
Gentle Teaching in a Violent Society	X				X
The Material vs. the Student					X

natural inclination is constantly to seek more effective teaching strategies, regardless of youngsters' backgrounds or the obstacles youngers face, have a fighting chance of becoming effective teachers of children in poverty. (1995, p. 53)

Another pronounced function for innovative STEM instruction is Real Teaching. There are many ways that STEM can be viewed and defined, it can appear to be complicated and complex because it embodies multiple disciplines and culturally responsive pedagogy. Time and available resources may also be problematic (National Research Council, 2011). Yet, Star Teachers can model project and problem-based work to nurture and revitalize the student's interest in STEM learning and careers. Stars constantly search for projects that will be of special interest to their students. Simply put, Star Teachers make learning "come alive." For example, national efforts have been in place to transform the mathematics classroom into one that embraces STEM education, learning communities, and inquiry-driven instruction, and moving away from traditional approaches, such as procedural knowledge and memorization of algorithms (Manouchehri, 2004). Although these national efforts have been supported and articulated by the NCTM, many urban, high-poverty school districts continue using the traditional route of teaching mathematics. According to Haberman (2010), the pedagogy of poverty dominates the classroom, and instructional practices are not consistent with the recommendations put forth by the NCTM. This, in turn, will impact STEM instruction and methodologies. McKinney et al. (2010) investigated the mathematics instructional practices of Star Teachers in urban, prevalent poverty schools. They concluded that Star Teachers use a variety of approaches and practices that are culturally relevant and support the NCTM's Principals and Standards (2000). These teaching practices include asking higher level questions; adding personal creativity; differentiating instruction; and using cooperative groups, manipulatives, hands-on, and problem-based learning activities (McKinney et al., 2013). They further examined the differences in the mathematics instructional practices between Star Teachers and those not so identified. Using a chi square test of independence, the results revealed that Star Teachers demonstrate those instructional practices advocated by the NCTM more frequently than those teachers not so identified. The data show significant differences between the two comparison groups in the frequency in which they utilize lecture, drill and practice, and the memorization of algorithms, procedures, and rules. Those teachers not identified as stars tended to employ these traditional instructional approaches more readily than stars (p. 809). According to Bransford et al. (1999) many urban students have trouble and failure when mathematics instruction is centered on abstract algorithms and procedures. Additionally, drill and practice and lecture do little in the preparation of students developing into analytical people and doers of mathematics (Berry, 2003; NCTM Principals and Standards, 2000; Van de Walle et al., 2023).

Many circumstances impact teaching and learning in urban, high-poverty schools. At best, STEM activities "can help teachers create a high performing classroom in which the teacher and student form a relationship-based learning community focused on innovation, creativity, achievement, self-mastery, and contributions to the community and society" (Soares & Vannest, 2013, p. 156).

Haberman (2005) states it best: "For children in poverty, succeeding in school is a matter of life and death. They cannot all be rock stars and sport figures. They must make it in school or spend their lives in hopelessness and desperation" (p. 152). However, Star Teachers have the ideology to "turn them on" to STEM careers.

4

Gender Bias in STEM Education

A father and son were in a terrible car accident. The father was killed instantly. The son was rushed to the emergency room. The surgeon runs in, takes one look at the boy and says, "I can't operate on this boy because this boy is my son!" How is this possible if the father was killed in the car accident?

If you didn't get this riddle right away, don't worry. You're not alone. Read it again. If you can't figure it out it's because your subconscious mind has eliminated a whole pool of people that would help you answer the riddle. What is the answer? The surgeon is the boy's mother. Whenever I (Berube) tell this riddle to a class full of college students, I get, "Is the surgeon the step-dad?" or "Is it the uncle?" Why don't many people get the correct answer at first? As I stated earlier, it's not a conscious decision on our parts to delete women from the equation. We know women doctors, lawyers, and engineers. We just don't really think it's "normal" yet for women to be in these fields. We view female doctors and such as "exceptional," and view their career choices as exceptions rather than the rule. We may even argue against this viewpoint, saying that it's ridiculous to suggest that women can't be these things. Ok, why then can't we get the riddle?

In the 1943 movie *Madame Curie*, Greer Garson and Walter Pidgeon portray Marie Curie and her husband Pierre Curie and the struggles they endured together in their quest to bring their (her) discovery of radium to the world. In one scene, they are seated before a university committee of professors and administrators (all men) while they beg for more and better laboratory space. They also have to justify the need for better facilities, and use Marie's work as the foundation for this justification. As the men on the panel question the Curies, the talk turns to how a woman could possibly warrant such high-level facilities, and how is it possible at all for her to be working on such things? Her husband, in full defense of his wife, says that "she is no ordinary woman" and deserves the space. In 1943, and indeed, in the early part of the 20th century, it wasn't shocking to hear those words pertaining to an intelligent woman. It wasn't thought odd either and was in fact part of the vocabulary of people everywhere in their *defense* of women for equality. Progressive thinking people referred to smart, ambitious women as extraordinary; with the unspoken idea being that average women still weren't cut out for science and intellectually hard work. Only now in the rear-view mirror do we see the bias in his statement.

The title of this chapter is "Gender Bias" for good reason. There is much research to suggest that there is still a bias against women; especially in STEM fields. Chang (2012) writes:

> Science professors at American universities widely regard female undergraduates as less competent than male students with the same accomplishments and skills, a new study by researchers at Yale concluded. As a result, the report found, the professors were less likely to offer the women mentoring or a job. And even if they were willing to offer a job, the salary was lower. The bias was pervasive, the scientists said, and probably reflected subconscious cultural influences rather than overt or deliberate discrimination" (p. D1).

Subconscious bias is more harmful than overt bias. If you don't know you are biased, then you are not actively trying to correct the bias.

Women and Higher Education

The Chronicle of Higher Education published The Gender Issue (November 2, 2012), devoted to looking at why there are differences between men and women in higher education, including STEM. According to Mangan (2012), there is a lopsided representation of women in engineering, with just 18% of undergraduate engineering degrees going to women, 22% of master's, and 23% doctoral. Education however, is another story. Women earn 80% of undergraduate degrees in education, 77% of master's, and

67% of doctoral degrees (p. B4). Why is this so? Mangan mentions a study conducted by Kristen Monroe, a professor of political science at the University of California at Irvine, which showed that a huge struggle most women face when climbing the career ladder is that integrating work and personal lives is extremely hard. Women still are responsible for most of the housework and child rearing, not to mention caretaking of elderly parents. "A critical problem in sciences or in any profession where you have to be in the office all day is that it's hard to have a job and raise children... my job as a political-science professor is much more flexible. I can teach courses while my kids are in school, stay up late, or sit at the computer and work while my daughter reads at the table near me. I couldn't do that if I were a doctor having to see patients or a research scientist responsible for a lab" (pp. B4, B5). Rosser and Taylor (2009) mirror this research, stating that many of the barriers women face are due to marriage and family creating demands and rules that are set forth by society that can derail a thriving STEM career.

Childcare in Europe for working women is light years ahead of American childcare. Most countries have on-site free childcare that enables moms to work in the same building that their child is being cared for. This creates great peace of mind and freedom for the mother to thrive at work. In an American Sociological AssociationClawson & Gerstel (2002) report that working parents in America struggle to find expensive yet mediocre daycare, while their European counterparts easily find numerous publicly funded programs offering good to excellent care. The only such programs in America are provided for the very poor, leaving working and middle class parents to find the funds for daycare on their own. The authors point to these differences between two European countries and America:

> European countries provide thought-provoking alternative models of child care. For example, focusing on differences between the systems available in France and Denmark, the authors find that French child care is intended primarily as early education and is open to all children, regardless of socioeconomic status. Almost 100 percent of French three-, four-, and five-year-olds are enrolled in the full-day, free écoles maternelles; all are part of the same national system, with the same curriculum, staffed by teachers paid good wages by the same national ministry. Denmark's child care system, on the other hand, offers a "nonschool model," and is intended to aid working parents, not educate children.
>
> The cost of the French child care is not cheap. However, in France, child care costs are considered to be a social responsibility and are publicly funded, while in the United States, parents themselves pay for these services. As Clawson and Gerstel remind us, not caring for our children is in the long term, and probably even in the short term, even more expensive. (Clawson & Gerstel, 2002, paras. 7, 8)

Basically the argument becomes one of belief systems: In America we believe in a capitalistic society where supply and demand dictate all services, even social. The word "socialism" has become such a bad word in America, that politicians are afraid to offer suggestions of models for childcare from more socialistic countries, *even when these models work*. So it really isn't about what works and what doesn't work. We already know what works. It's about what we value in America. Christopher Hitchens used to say that the cure for poverty is the empowerment of women, and supportive childcare would be a major step in ensuring workplace security and financial equality.

Monroe (2012) argues that while the practical navigations of life make it harder for women to succeed in the sciences, there is also "a lot of implicit prejudice" (para. 14). Administrators tend to see women as not being able to devote 100% of their energies to the job. Donna Nelson, a professor of chemistry at the University of Oklahoma, agrees: "Women's input isn't always valued as highly as men's when it comes to important matters" (para. 18). Monroe mentions the famous study by researchers at the University of Pennsylvania's Wharton School of Business which found that professors in a variety of disciplines were much less likely to be responsive to communication from women or minority applicants to doctoral programs, and that the problem was worse in academic disciplines that tend to pay more (para. 22). A Yale study found that science professors at American universities viewed female undergraduates as less competent than their equally-qualified male peers, and that the professors (female included) tended to favor male candidates for positions as lab managers when they were given identical applications with either male or female names. The male students were also offered higher salaries and more mentoring (para. 21).

The Importance of Role Models and Mentors

All fields of human endeavor have networks that have to be successfully navigated in order to be able to "make it" in the field. These networks include mentors; people who have seniority to the people seeking to enter the field, and who are in positions to help, guide, and tutor the neophyte in the tricks of the trade. Does subconscious or even overt bias exist in the mentoring process? According to research, mentoring is vital when it comes to successful outcomes for junior professionals. Dunbar and Kinnersley (2011) state that their study

> supported earlier research and confirmed the importance of mentoring relationships for women who aspire to administrative positions. These findings suggest that institutions of higher education, professional associations, and

graduate programs that prepare women to become administrators should develop methods to promote the culture of mentoring. (p. 17)

Who is mentoring these women in academia? The best mentors are senior level faculty and administrators, and there is no shortage of them for male to male mentoring. Bilen-Grene et al. (2008) state:

> A recent study by the American Association of University Professors (AAUP) piques interest in the current role of women in higher education. The examination of 1,445 colleges and universities reveals that while women earn more than half of all PhD degrees granted to American citizens today, they still comprise only about 45% of tenure-track faculty, 31% of tenured faculty, and just 24% of full professorships in 2005–2006 (West & Curtis, 2006). More women than men are in part-time or non-tenure track positions, and the increasing scarcity of women as you look at higher academic ranks is clearly shown. Participation of women is lowest in the doctoral-granting institutions, where women constitute just 34% of full-time faculty, 26% of tenured faculty, and 19% of full professors. (p. 1)

So if 75% to 80% of all senior faculty are male, and almost half of all new PhDs and faculty are women, then you have a mentoring problem. Especially before the women are even hired. These women should be mentored before they graduate with their doctorates. These women are clearly not climbing up the academic ladder.

Since women holding STEM positions in higher education may be the only women in their departments, outside sources for mentoring are needed. Karukstis (2010) states:

> Senior women faculty, like female students, often prefer mentors who are like themselves because they perceive such female role models to have experienced professional and personal difficulties and challenges similar to their own (Simeone, 1987; Packard, 1999; Chesler & Chesler, 2002). Yet, since there are few women faculty in high-ranking positions, cross-gender mentoring is likely to be the only traditional mentoring option available for senior women faculty in science and engineering at a given institution. To remedy the lack of access to experienced female mentors, alternative modes of mentoring must be found. (p. 35)

To remedy this she suggests a "horizontal" mentoring strategy:

> These faculty members represented the only senior women chemists at their institutions and, in some cases, the only female chemists at any rank in their departments. In most cases they were the first women faculty hired in their departments so they had few, if any, female role models in their institution as they progressed through tenure and promotion to full professor. Thus,

peer mentoring involving *external* mentors was a logical approach for this group of women faculty. The varied career experiences and achievements of this cohort of women faculty provided a rich resource of guidance and recommendations. (p. 35)

A person could assume that a place like Harvard would be less likely to engage in sexism than a less enlightened place. But at a conference in 2005, no less than the Harvard president himself—Lawrence Summers—made a statement that not only rocked the academic world, but forced his resignation to boot. Referring to why elite institutions have so few tenured women scientists and engineers on their faculties, he said that the underrepresentation of women in STEM fields is due to "different availability of aptitude at the high end," and less likely due to patterns of discrimination and socialization. Summers also suggested that women are unwilling or unable to work the long hours necessary for success in science in top-tier institutions such as Harvard (Rosser & Taylor, 2009).

Mentoring is not just for university faculty members. Platz (2012) describes the "IGNITE" program:

A partnership of professional women working in STEM careers, who volunteer their time to mentor young women in high-school about opportunities for them in STEM. These high-school girls don't know many women in STEM fields, and have no role models to look up to for advice and guidance. IGNITE has impacted more than 20,000 girls over the past 10 years, and the presence of the program in the Seattle School District has seen enrollment in STEM classes jump from 10% to 50%. (p. 27)

Stereotypes of STEM scientists permeate American society, but are especially hard on women. Platz (2012) cites another study by Auletta, who writes:

"Several female computer-science majors at Stanford pointed to the depiction of women in films like *The Social Network*, where the boys code and the girls dance around in their underwear." IGNITE is working to counteract these stereotypes. (p. 29)

The moral of IGNITE's story is that it doesn't take much to shatter stereotypes and excite young girls about the amazing opportunities that STEM careers can provide. (p. 29)

Carol Gilligan is a leading scholar in feminist studies. A few years ago I was fortunate enough to interview Dr. Gilligan for a study I was conducting and a book my husband was writing that included Gilligan as the topic of a chapter (Berube, 2000). We met in her office at Harvard where she held the title of Professor of Psychology (in 2002 she moved to New York University where she holds joint positions in the School of Education and the School of Law). Gilligan wrote a seminal book in gender studies in 1982 entitled *In a Different Voice*. The book explains how girls see and talk about the world, and how it is different from how boys do it. She told me that girls are very confident, outspoken, and bossy in elementary school, and everyone who has known an elementary aged girl can attest to that. But sometime in early adolescence (middle school), girls "lose their voices" metaphorically because they are trying to fit in, don't want to stand out and especially, don't want to turn off boys in their classes. They fall off the "table" and scholastically this can alter academic trajectory. This has implications in math and science classes, where a smart girl may refrain from raising her hand and answering questions for fear that she may appear smarter than the boy she is trying to gain the attention of sitting in the next row. (This is not dissimilar to Ogbu's 1986 "Acting White" study, which posits that some gifted African-American male students in a Washington DC school did not live up to their talents and abilities for fear of "acting White" and for being accused of selling out by their friends [Fordham & Ogbu, 1986].)

Tan and Calabrese-Barton (2008) mention research on middle school girls and what happens to them:

> Middle school is an especially crucial time to examine how girls, like Melanie, take up science in the classroom in ways that matter to them. Middle school is, after all, a time when girls' choices of peer groups, self-selected mentors, school grades, and after-school programs play a pivotal role in the high school trajectories they pursue and in supporting their efforts to become and remain engaged in science (AAUW, 1992; Lee, 2002; Malcolm, 1997). Middle school is also a time when girls' attitude toward science and achievement in science drop precipitously (Atwater et al., 1995). (p. 568)

Identity and Science

Identity formation is the process whereby a person creates a sense of self over time. This includes personality features, likes, dislikes, and who we think we are. It becomes our vantage point in the world, and can inform our decisions as we go through life. It is also called individuation. There are several theories of identity formation, including Erikson's (1950) theory of psychosocial development. Yet, very little has been written on females and identity; especially in science. Historically, researchers and scientists have thought of the masculine viewpoint on psychological issues as *the* viewpoint; the *normal* prototype, including the famous "Stages of Moral Development" put forth by Gilligan's senior colleague, Lawrence Kohlberg. Kohlberg used the "Heinz dilemma" to highlight how his subjects (boys) would handle a moral issue. A man named Heinz has a wife who is dying and he needs a certain drug in order to save her life; however, he can't afford the druggist's price. What does he do? Does he steal the drug? Would that be right or wrong? Most boys and men would say that either he shouldn't steal the drug, because then he would go to jail, or that yes he should because it would save a life. Gilligan asked girls the same question and they came up with different answers. The man should barter with the druggist; maybe trade work for the drugs. This way, the *relationship* with the druggist would be preserved, and he would also have the life-saving drug (Kohlberg, 1958; Gilligan, 1982).

Kohlberg only used male subjects in this study and extrapolated the findings to the general population, a fact that did not escape Gilligan who went on to later create her own gender-based theory. Gilligan's moral development theory included "an ethic of caring" that was different from the "ethic of justice" found in Kohlberg's work. Gilligan knew that relationships were vitally important to women, and that the way women view the world can be just and moral; sometimes without the punitive nature of a justice mentality. The way men and women and boys and girls view the world may be different based on the situation. If we expand this thinking to a middle school science class, we may find that in male dominated areas of life (science, technology, engineering, math), girls may not "identify" with science. Science may not be a part of the feminine identity. Tan and Calabrese-Barton (2008) cite research by Sadker and Sadker (1995):

> Yet we know that traditionally girls are positioned with less power in the science classroom. They are called on less often to answer content questions and not given as much attention as the boys by the teacher. As a result of this "hidden curriculum," girls are led to believe that a scientific identity is antagonistic with their gendered identity (Sadker & Sadker, 1995). This further illustrates the importance of understanding how girls author their identities in practice while they learn. (p. 570)

Park et al. (2011) suggest that women distance themselves from STEM when their goal to be romantically desirable becomes activated because pursuing intelligence goals in masculine domains (i.e., STEM) conflicts with pursuing romantic goals associated with traditional romantic scripts and gender norms. Consistent with the hypothesis, women—but not men—who viewed images or overheard conversations related to romantic goals reported less positive attitudes towards STEM and less preference for majoring in math/science compared to other disciplines. It seems that not much changes as girls grow into women in many cases.

Sapna and Plant (2010) agree that social factors play a part in precluding women's interest in the STEM field computer programming. They point out that all academic fields possess certain prototypes with perceived traits and attributes (Turner et al., 1987), and the extent to which a person's own perceived traits and attributes overlaps with these academic prototypes are related to improved attitudes toward the field (Hannover & Kessels, 2004; Lee, 1998; Rommes et al., 2007, p. 476). The authors hypothesized that students' expectations about whether or not they could be successful in computer science and certain social identity threats (the presence of potential threats to one's identity) would affect a lack of interest in the computer science field. Specifically: "Thus, we predict that women's perceptions of themselves as dissimilar from computer scientists relative to men will predict their lower interest in the field" (Sapna & Plant, 2010, p. 476), and "we hypothesize that women will perceive less similarity between themselves and computer scientists than men will perceive" (Sapna & Plant, 2010, p. 476). Upon conducting a Manova to test for gender difference on all variables, there were significant effects; compared to men, women reported less interest in computer science, and perceived less similarity to computer science majors. Women reported greater social identity threats in computer science in the form of more sexism, more stereotype threat, and lower gender valuation. Women also reported lower expectations of success in computer science than men (Sapna & Plant, 2010, p. 481). This is not to say that women's perceptions are the only reason for STEM disparities, but this may be a contributing factor.

Morganson et al. (2010) examine "social coping" to explain the gender gap. Social coping is a tool that enables individuals to deal with challenges and problems in their environments (p. 170). The authors' goal was to explain the underrepresentation of women in STEM fields and to provide guidance for career development. They report that women and men deal with stressors differently; men either ignore or try to change the stressor, women use social groups or support (social coping) in order to deal with stressors. They also report that women use social coping more than men (p. 171). They examined coping as a mechanism both for understanding and for addressing the retention issue concerning undergraduates with a STEM major. The authors expected the use of social coping to enable individuals to overcome barriers, and increase commitment, persistence, and performance—especially in women. They were also interested in the point at which individuals intend to withdraw from their majors. Both commitment and turnover intent are considered persistence outcomes (p. 171). Their findings showed that women do use social coping more than men do, and that social coping was a significant predictor of commitment and persistence outcomes (p. 173). Even though persistence and commitment are affective domains, these results are important, because when "women leave STEM majors, they have higher grades in college than men who leave; but women report greater dissatisfaction with their majors more than men do" (Adelman, 1998 as cited in Morganson et al, 2010, p. 176).

Girls' Identity in Urban Science Classrooms

Just as Marie Curie struggled to make her voice heard in the male dominated world of early 20th century chemistry, the same is true for modern girls seeking to find a welcoming place in the science classroom. When discussing science identity, nowhere does this become more complicated than when you combine race and gender as factors in urban science classrooms. If science is the domain of White males, then how are females of color going to develop identities that include science and STEM? Tan and Calabrese-Barton (2008) cite Brickhouse and Potter (2001) who conducted research on urban girls in science classrooms. These girls are struggling to belong and to find an accepting place in the world. Much of the time they are marginalized in all areas of life:

> Their work reveals that through the experiences of marginalization in the science classroom and even in peer groups, urban girls learn that membership in a school science community is often impossible or undesirable. Having a science or technology-related identity does not mean that one will necessarily succeed in school, if that science-related identity does not also reflect the values of school-mediated engagement or if students do not have access to the resources they need to do science well. However, successful participation in school science or technology, despite a lack of resources in the home environment, can be better facilitated when students have a science-related identity they can draw upon. Brickhouse and Potter's study is important because it raises questions about how to help students retain an identity that is desirable to them in their home communities, yet also allow them to cross the boundaries of race, class, and gender, to get access to a science culture that too often resides only in more privileged communities. (p. 570)

How can teachers ensure that all girls, including girls of color, are included at the table of STEM? Teachers can purposefully work an individual student's identity and personality into the science classroom, and can make a point of creating an environment where discourse is inclusive. If the teacher controls the atmosphere of the classroom whereby allowing a student's personal experiences with science into the classroom, then deliberate connections are made between the student's world and the world of science (Reveles et al., 2004). Race and STEM have been discussed in Chapter 3, but the combination of race and gender can prove to be a fatal blow for STEM education if not recognized and dealt with by talented teachers armed with culturally sensitive pedagogy and a supportive community.

This chapter began with a riddle; the answer being that a surgeon was a woman. While we know that women are surgeons, it has not yet become part of the "feminine identity" as it has for men. If a person is describing his or her surgeon, if the surgeon was a man they will just say "the surgeon was great." However, if the surgeon was a woman, the person is more likely to say "the woman surgeon was great." It is still unusual for women to be surgeons. The same would hold true for a pilot or a mechanic. These have not yet become part of the feminine gestalt. It is a subconscious construct that we all fall victim to. Some may argue that you can't force women into a field that they are not interested in; this is the argument that the cognitive scientist Steven Pinker makes. In 2005 Harvard University hosted a debate between Pinker and another cognitive scientist, Elizabeth Spelke, concerning the raging controversy over President Lawrence Summer's comments on the ability of women in STEM. It was entitled "The Science of Gender and Science: Pinker vs. Spelke: a Debate" (2005). Pinker argued the "nature" side and Spelke defended the "nurture" side to explain differences. Pinker argued the "people vs. things" belief that women are naturally more interested in people than things. He also argued that men and women have different vocational interests and you can't force women to go into science fields if they don't want to. For the sake of argument, if Pinker has a point, does it matter if women are choosing to stay out of STEM, or actively avoiding it? Maybe the question needs to be why? Whichever side you agree with, the end result is that there are too few women in STEM, and half the human population deserves to find out why.

Slowing Down Scientific Progress

The argument can also be made that if women were equal partners in scientific endeavor, then humankind would be at least twice as advanced as we are today. Billions of human minds are not engaging in the scientific discussion. Billions of good ideas wasted because society does not support the one holding the idea. Indeed, if we examine what it takes to create brilliance, we will discover that women are in higher possession of these qualities than men.

When Einstein's mind flashed on his idea that time was variable and the speed of light was constant (later to become special relativity), he was daydreaming in his patent office; gazing out of the window at the clock tower across the square. He had been working as a patent clerk after graduation from university. He could not find a job as a professor; he was so far advanced that the professors interviewing him thought he was crazy. He was proposing ideas that went against their ways of thinking. He struggled for 2 years to find an academic job, and in depressed desperation settled on a patent clerk position in Bern Switzerland. He did patent work on electrical and mechanical synchronization of time, so he was already thinking of time and space and how they were connected.

In this particular daydream, he pictured himself riding a beam of light and realized that if another person was riding a beam of light next to him, they would both look stationary. This sort of thinking requires several things:

- peace
- quiet
- intense concentration
- lack of distractions
- long stretches of time
- energy
- self-absorption
- creativity

Upon examination of these requirements, one can notice that this deep thinking requires a substantial investment in solitude and time. When can women who are juggling children have this sort of luxury? Read any one of these on the list and you will see how impossible it is for women neck deep in childcare to be able to engage in one of them, let alone all of them. Brian Greene is a professor of mathematics and physics at Columbia University. He is also working on string theory, the emerging atomic theory that promises to unite quantum physics with gravitational and astrophysics, and would become, if successful, the famous "theory of everything" that physicists have been struggling with for over a century. I attended a lecture he gave a few years ago in New York City. A member of the audience asked him what an average day looks like for him, and he responded that a very important part of his work includes "sitting and thinking," alone, in his office. He said that when he is doing this, it appears that he is not doing anything, and has to be firm with protecting this lest anyone think that he is wasting valuable research time. Great insights and ideas have been birthed in studies such as his all across the world, and the nurturing soil is peace, quiet, and solitude. Deep, focused thought; the type that produces great works of science, mathematics, indeed any human endeavor, cannot survive otherwise.

Connections

Let's concentrate on the last item on the list: creativity. According to Kotler (2012), "From a neurological perspective, creativity is the product of the brain making long distance connections" (para. 9). According to Steve Jobs (1996),

> Creativity is just connecting things. When you ask creative people how they did something, they feel a little guilty because they didn't really do it, they just saw something. It seemed obvious to them after a while. That's because they were able to connect experiences they've had and synthesize new things. And the reason they were able to do that was that they've had more experiences or they have thought more about their experiences than other people. (Mcmanamy, 2011, para. 1)

Brains that are good at making connections all have something in common, more white matter. White matter serves to connect different processing parts of the brain. Women have ten times the amount of white matter than men do, and white matter represents the networking of—or connections between—these processing centers. Brains that make connections have more white matter (Haier et al., 2005).

It would seem from a strictly scientific viewpoint that women would be more apt to make the giant scientific discoveries than men would be, if only women had the resources, time, peace, quiet, support, energy, and ability to focus on one thing for a long period of time as men do. If scientists such as Pinker declare that the brains of men and women are indeed different, then it stands to reason that women are uniquely built for science, and that the propensity for creativity and connections favors the female brain.

Einstein's Brain

It can be argued using logic that Einstein's brain was more "feminine" than the average scientist's at the time. A post-mortem dissection of Einstein's brain by pathologist Thomas S. Harvey at the University of Pennsylvania shortly after Einstein's death in 1955 uncovered a startling discovery. Among the peculiarities found included a reduced Sylvian fissure, the large fold in the brain that separates the frontal lobes, and a 15% larger than average inferior parietal lobe, which is responsible for mathematical thought, visuospatial cognition, and imagery of movement (Hotz, 2005). This is important because Einstein told all who would listen that he thought in pictures and was a visual learner.

Since the original autopsy, Einstein's brain had been under the careful watch of Dr. Harvey, but in 1980, Dr. Marian C. Diamond, a neuroanatomist at the University of California, Berkeley, persuaded Dr. Harvey to give her sections of Einstein's brain. It took 3 years for her to convince Harvey to send her the tissue samples. Dr. Diamond wanted to take samples from the brains of 11 men and compare the numbers of glial cells found to the amount in Einstein's brain. She already had the samples from the 11 men, now she just needed Einstein's brain. Here, Dr. Diamond (1999) describes when she finally received the samples:

> In a mayonnaise jar filled with fluid, here were my four sugarcube-size pieces of Einstein's brain. Evidently, Harvey had cut up the brain and embedded the pieces in a substance called celloidin which harden almost like plastic. Having the brain in this condition was ideal for my purposes because we wanted to count cells under the microscope. To do this it was necessary to make thin slices, 6 micra in thickness (a micron is one thousandth of a millimeter). In order to cut at this precise level of thickness the tissue had to be processed in celloidin. Preserving the brain in this manner does not allow for some other methods of examination such as refined chemical analysis. We were extremely fortunate to have the tissue preserved in a way that proved ideal for us. We had our 44 pieces of brain from the 11 normal males. We could now compare the glial neuron ratios in the 4 pieces from Einstein's brain with the 44 pieces from the normal males. With the help of an excellent technician and statistician (a scientist rarely works alone), we learned that in all four areas, Einstein had more glial cells per neuron than the average man, but in only the left inferior parietal area did he have statistically significantly more. (para. 22)

Before the experiment, Diamond (1999) had hypothesized that "since the number of glial cells per neuron increases as one ascends the phylogenetic tree, I reasoned that the more highly evolved area in the human brain should have more glial cells per neuron" (para 4). Einstein's brain had a statistically significant higher number of glial cells. White matter consists mostly of glial cells and axons used for transmittal of signals from across the brain. Women's brains have 30% more white matter than men. So Einstein had the same brain properties that women have; a larger amount of white matter—brain tissue used to make "connections." In other words, Einstein had a highly evolved brain; equal to that of the average woman.

Gender Bias in STEM Education • 45

In 1994 Herrnstein and Murray published a controversial book entitled *The Bell Curve*, which sought to tease apart how IQ and intelligence affected and are affected by class structure, socioeconomic status, and race. It was and is controversial because they defend the "nature" viewpoint that human brains and IQs differ from race to race and person to person, and that these differences are fixed. Not much is mentioned concerning gender, but there is one notation concerning variation in IQ scores among men and women.

If we look at a picture of the typical "bell-curve" for IQ scores, we see that the mean is 100 (See Figure 4.1). (A bell-curve is the statistical result of taking a number of individual scores, and finding the average. The highest point on the "bell" is the average scores for the population being studied.)

Herrnstein and Murray (1994) make the argument that when it comes to gender, men and women have identical IQs; however,

> men have a broader distribution. In the NSLY (National Longitudinal Survey of Youth), for example, women had a mean on the Armed Forces Qualification Test (AFQT) that was .06 standard deviation lower than the male mean and a standard deviation that was .11 narrower. For the Wechsler Intelligence Scale for Children, the average boy tests 1.8 IQ points higher than the average girl, and boys have a standard deviation that is .8 point larger than girls. The larger variation among men means that there are more men than women at either extreme of the IQ distribution. (p. 275)

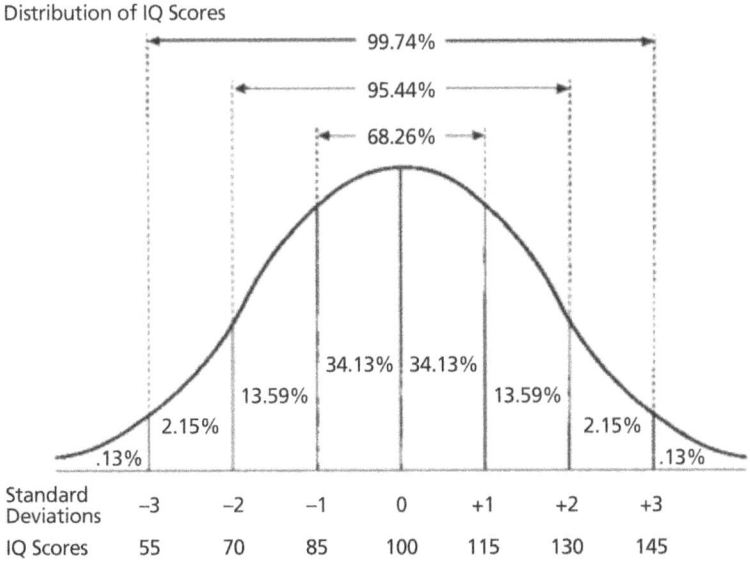

Figure 4.1 "Sense and Nonsense About IQ." *Source:* Locurto, 1991, p. 5.

The fact that there are more male "outliers" is not surprising. More males than females suffer from disorders such as attention deficit disorder, mental retardation, autism, and other cognitive disabilities, which would explain those outliers skewed to the left of the bell curve. More males than females sit at the higher edges of the IQ bell curve too, and this is understandable if examined in the context of this discussion. When talent and ability are nurtured and rewarded, they are strengthened. Nurturing creates opportunities for intellectual growth, which can be measured on an IQ test. As was mentioned earlier... attaining the highest echelons of the scientific or mathematic community—tenured professors, researchers, Nobel Prize winners—requires a certain behavioral set. Someone has mentored these folks, taught them the "dance steps" of their field. These exceptional scientists are afforded the luxury of peace, quiet, intense concentration, lack of distractions, long stretches of time, energy, self-absorption, and finally, when you have all of these, you can then make creative contributions to your field and maybe even wind up in the history (his-story) books.

5

The Effects of No Child Left Behind and High-Stakes Testing on STEM Education

In 2004 I (Berube) wrote an article entitled "Are Standards Preventing Good Teaching?" (Berube, 2004). In this article I described a study I conducted with eighth grade science students in Norfolk Virginia Public Schools. Towards the end of the school year in Virginia, students from across the state take their annual Virginia Standards of Learning (SOL) tests in their grade levels and content areas. For eighth grade science students, this would be the eighth grade science SOL. There had been much talk about rising test scores in science across the state of Virginia (Virginia Department of Education, 2001). My goal was to see how reliable this gain was; since I suspected that there was more to the story than rising test scores.

I constructed a version of the SOL test the eighth grade science students had taken a week earlier, during May of 2001. My test was called the "Comprehension Measurement," since it sought to measure actual comprehension instead of multiple choice test-taking skill. It was the same exact SOL test they had just taken, but after each multiple choice answer, I asked them to explain or defend their answers with a short simple statement. I then took the students who passed the SOL test with a 400 or higher, and then compared their scores from their SOL exams to my Comprehension Measurement scores. What I found was shocking. 71% of the students who *passed* the eighth grade science SOL failed the Comprehension Measurement. The students were passing the standardized test, but could not explain what they had just done. No deep learning had taken place.

On May 11, 2012, the local Norfolk Virginia newspaper, *The Virginian-Pilot*, published a story entitled "Va. 8th-Graders Show Improved Science Ability" (Sampson, 2012). The article starts "Virginia's eighth-graders outperform their peers nationwide in science, but only 40 percent show a solid grasp of the subject, according to a national report released Thursday" (Sampson, 2012, p. A3). This reinforces the findings of my study, that the students could pass the test, but not comprehend the content.

High-Stakes Tests

Much has been written about high-stakes tests and the negative impact such tests have on students of color (Horn, 2003; Madaus & Clarke, 2001; Steele & Aronson, 1995), girls (Rebhorn & Miles, 1999; AAUW Report, 1995), students with disabilities (Figlio & Getzler, 2002; Phillips, 2009), and second language learners (Lim, 2010; Russell & Kavanaugh, 2011). Many standardized tests are punitive in nature, and may damage the very school systems they claim to be helping (Berube, 2008b, p. 86). The "accountability" movement, birthed from the No Child Left Behind legislation pushed upon schools during George W. Bush's presidency, sought to make teachers accountable for the woes of the failing American school system. Many blamed teachers unions and the teachers themselves for every single negative outcome. While no one wants to keep bad teachers in classrooms, and while everyone agrees that teachers should meet standards and be accountable for them, no one was prepared for the fallout from NCLB that would rain down on superintendents, principals, and teachers. Failing to meet these guidelines could mean closing a beloved school, or the withdrawal of funds desperately needed. So the easiest target for "change" was the individual teacher.

Many people confuse assessment with accountability, which are actually separate ideas. Education in America has become all about accountability and assessment. Assessment should actually be diagnostic in nature, not punitive. The very notion of punitive assessment goes against the very grain of what education is supposed to stand for. It would be the equivalent of showing up sick at the doctor's office and receiving a tongue lashing instead of your treatment or prescription. As a result of this atmosphere, a culture of cheating has been created and is thriving in school districts all across America. A recent newspaper article from *The Virginian-Pilot* in Norfolk Virginia states:

> Remember when teachers put the fear of God into you about cheating? You'd be huddled over your desk with arms bowed out in a circle protecting your test paper from the wandering eyes of a potential cheater. If you didn't and cheating occurred and the teacher couldn't determine which one of the identically or nearly identically filled out papers belonged to the cheater, you'd both wind up failing. Worse, the teacher would tell your parents. The Atlanta testing scandal and an emerging one in Philadelphia—plus a slew of others that have gone underreported or unacknowledged publicly—have upended that scared-straight classroom picture. Today, the litany of revelations and allegations of how some teachers have aided and engaged in test cheating themselves is the scary part. Recent reports that a whopping 178 Atlanta Public Schools teachers and principals—82 of whom have confessed of cheating—has grabbed the headlines. Now Philadelphia has taken the spotlight. An investigation is under way after a state study showed 89 schools across the state, including 28 in the city, had been flagged for questionable gains on test scores. But these high-profile cases are only the tip of the iceberg. For more than a decade charges of test cheating have dogged cities and states nationwide. Among them? Washington DC; Arizona; California; Colorado, Florida; Maryland; Michigan; New Jersey; New York; Ohio; and Texas, as well as Pennsylvania and Georgia. (Flono, 2011, p. 7)

The Politics of Science Education

Education has been a political football for generations. Progressives and their Dewey inspired public schools are mostly democrats; while choice and privatization advocates are mostly republicans. Big government has traditionally been the enemy of the right, but when George W. Bush implemented No Child Left Behind in 2001 the thought was that accountability would help to solve the problems in education, through an expansion of government in the area of public education. Much of this accountability would come from test scores. These scores would show us which teachers and administrators were doing their jobs properly, and which were not. NCLB was a reauthorization of the Elementary and Secondary Education Act, which required assessments be developed to measure basic skills for all students, including "disadvantaged." Funding for schools would rest on the outcome of the tests, thereby turning the assessments into high-stakes tests, instead of the simple measurement instruments they were meant to be. High-stakes tests are game changers for public education in that they can literally close a school down, forcing students to go elsewhere. The right has not traditionally been friendly to the urban poor, and really has no personal stake in seeing them succeed.

The idea behind NCLB (2001) was a decent one however; to raise standards and accountability. Schools that scored below a certain point would receive help in order to bring themselves up to par. However, it was never funded fully so as to implement many of the "prescriptive" tools that many failing schools needed in order to survive. What happened was that these failing schools were shut down instead of being helped to improve. Some of the most damage caused by punitive testing is to STEM subjects. Mathematics takes patience to learn, and patience to teach well. Science should be a creative endeavor, and creativity is not best measured by close-ended bubble tests. When teachers "teach to the test," there is no room for creative responses from students and ideas that are not similar to what is on the test. Where do new ideas and innovation fit into a standardized test?

With the advent of No Child Left Behind (2001), politicians had to come up with a way to access these new "standards"; one that would show to the country how they in turn were accountable to the voters. It should be noted that politicians, not educators, were left to implement these sanctions on school districts that were failing these assessments. Many of these state tests, like the Virginia SOLs had already been in place and given to students each year, but with NCLB they became high-stakes tests, where teachers could lose jobs, schools could lose funding, and principals could be transferred. Worse yet, states could shutter schools.

The closing of neighborhood schools in turn has a disastrous effect on real estate values, neighborhood identification, and quality of life issues; so teachers—pressured by principals—will do anything to avoid the pink slip. It is a vicious cycle. According to Flono (2001):

> Proponents of high-stakes testing prefer to deny it, but this teacher-aided kind of cheating has grown exponentially with the advent of the No Child Left Behind law. The law focused on test scores as the core measure of student progress, using those scores to label schools as good or bad, and threatening loss of funding or other punitive measures if students aren't proficient—based on a test score—in math and reading by 2014. (para. 7)

Of course, teachers still need to prepare students for these tests, and there are research-based techniques to ensure success in this area. The key would be for the teacher to not teach solely "to the test," but to prepare the students for the test in meaningful ways. This topic will be fully discussed in Chapter 8.

What happens when the city leadership sits in their suburban homes—along with the politicians and community leaders—as the urban schools are closed down? The issue is very black or white (no pun intended) for these powerful middle-class politicians: the poor people don't care about education, they don't follow the rules for success, they don't take advantage of the education in their neighborhood schools. They think it is their duty to protect their children and communities from people like that—people who can't seemingly get their acts together enough to even graduate from high school. The tests are simple enough, they think. Pay attention, study, pass the test, then your school will be fine—secure. Fire the teachers who can't get their kids to pass the test, hire ones who can. Close the neighborhood school if necessary, it's no skin of our noses. Who cares if real estate values go down ever further? It's not happening in our backyards, and we won't let it happen, because we are better, more deserving apparently. Our students pass the tests; they study and pay attention and the fault must be solely with the teacher and student, but mostly the teacher. So the myth continues.

In Chicago City Public Schools in 2012, a massive teacher strike made the news. They were mainly fighting Rahm Emmanuel against teacher evaluations based solely on high-stakes tests, and lack of resources. How can they be held totally accountable with no resources with which to teach? The left has an honorable history concerning labor unions, including the AFT (American Federation of Teachers), the NEA (National Education Association), the UFT (United Federation of Teachers), and the CTU (Chicago Teachers Union)—a local of the AFT. The left sees strikes as a democratic tool when all else fails. They see unions as necessary organizations that ensure that management can't take advantage of their workforce. Unions have given Americans 40-hour work weeks, benefits, safe working conditions, child-labor laws, and a host of other protections. Union workers strike (walk off the job) as a result of perceived unfair practices; including pay issues, policy (such as the CTU members in Chicago protesting firing of teachers over high-stakes test scores), and a host of other issues. The left sees this as a democratic right of Americans to "own" their country, as opposed to the elite bosses and the few in charge.

The right, on the other hand, view unions as the organizations of crybaby loafers, who would shove children under the bus in order to get higher pensions. Lazy, incompetent teachers must be the problem with American schools, and if only we could fire these lazy malcontents at will, the schools would improve. Urban myths of suspended teachers holed up in art rooms sleeping and eating doughnuts all day while collecting paychecks still circulate among these groups. Unions must be abolished and teachers must not be allowed to get "tenure," that golden ticket to Lazyville.

The Effects of High-Stakes Testing on Minorities

Claude Steele published famous articles on the effects of high-stakes testing on populations with a lot to lose. In Steele and Aronson's 1995 paper "A Threat in the Air: How Stereotypes Shape Intellectual Identity and Performance" he produced evidence that test results can be misleading if the threat of stereotype is introduced. Stereotype threat is an anxiety or concern in a situation where the person has the potential to confirm a negative stereotype about their social group. Steele (1997) defines it as "the social-psychological threat that arises when one is in a situation or doing something for which a negative stereotype about one's group applies" (p. 614). Steele gave the GRE (graduate school exam) to two groups that had been admitted to Stanford University—African-Americans and Whites—but said nothing special about the test beforehand. The two groups were equal in intelligence. The assumption was that the test was real and that it would count. The African-American group did not do as well as Whites. Steele then split the group into three sub-groups: a stereotype threat group that were told that the test was a measure of their intelligence, a non-stereotype threat group that was told the test was a laboratory problem-solving task non-indicative of their intelligence, and a third condition who were told to judge the test on difficulty, but was non-indicative of their intelligence. The results were drastically different (see Figure 5.1). This time the African-Americans in the non-stereotype threat treatment groups improved their scores a statistically significant amount (adjusted for previous SAT scores).

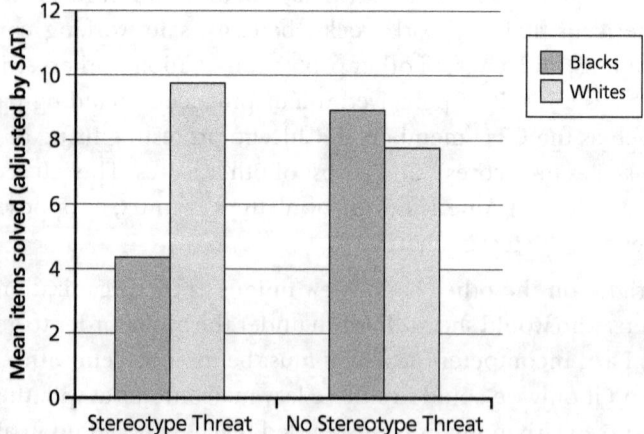

Figure 5.1 The effects of stereotype threat on the standardized test performance of college students (adjusted for group differences on SAT). *Source:* Aronson et al., 1998, p. 405.

The brain cannot simultaneously worry about performance and actually perform well.

NCLB and the Poorest of the Poor Minority Urban Students

Speaking of the racial gap, how has NCLB affected the poorest of the poor minority students?

A surprising, unexpected, and arguably one of the few benefits of NCLB, has been the focus on the poorest students, where there was none before. One of the most controversial discoveries of NCLB policy has been that the poorest classrooms in America are finally getting some sort of attention. In terms of adequate yearly progress, Kolodziej (2011) notes that "focuses on the importance AYP places on minority students has given much needed attention to these students who need better quality education" (p. 59). Also, the goals and requirements set by NCLB are

> without a doubt, a noble intention to improve the education of all students: NCLB "holds [public] schools...accountable for raising the achievement of all students, particularly those with disabilities, those from low-income families and racial and ethnic minorities, and those with limited English proficiency. (CQ Press, 2005, p. 469)

National Assessment of Educational Progress

In 1969, the National Center for Education Statistics ([NCES]; housed within the Institute of Education Sciences of the U.S. Department of Education), authorized a project titled the

> National Assessment of Educational Progress (NAEP), that periodically conducts assessments in American public schools in reading, math, science, writing, U.S. history, civics, geography, and other subjects (Science 2011; National Assessment of Educational Progress at Grade 8). This congressionally mandated project was dubbed "the Nation's Report Card"; the findings inform the public about the academic achievement of elementary and secondary students in the United States. (Science 2011; National Assessment of Educational Progress at Grade 8)

In 2001, when No Child Left Behind was passed, changes in how the state-run tests were implemented were put into place. Each state that received Title I funding was now required to take the reading and math tests in Grades 4 and 8 every 2 years. Subjects like science and writing remain voluntary.

The sample for the 2012 science NAEP assessment included 122,000 eighth-graders in American public schools. The NAEP science assessment measures knowledge and abilities in the areas of physical, earth, life, and space science. Findings show that scores increased from an average of 150 in 2009 to an average of 152 in 2011. And although the percentage of students scoring at or above Basic and Proficient levels rose in 2011, the percentage of students scoring at the Advanced level showed no improvement (see Figure 5.2).

In effect, this means that only one third of American science students can be said to be competent in science. Most of America's science students are mediocre. Sadly, only 2% are advanced. There was a 35 point gap between White and African-American students. Not surprisingly, males also scored higher than females; average scores for boys were 5 points higher in science than for girls. Socioeconomic status mattered too. Students on free or reduced lunch (45% of American 8th grade students) scored 27 points lower than students not eligible for free or reduced-price lunch.

Private school students scored higher than public school students; scoring 12 points higher.

It is worth noting that private schools always seem to out-score public schools on standardized testing (see Figure 5.3). Lubienski and Lubienski (2005) reported this discrepancy: "Public school students scored lower on

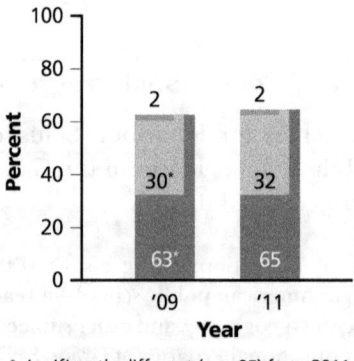

* significantly different (*p* < .05) from 2011.

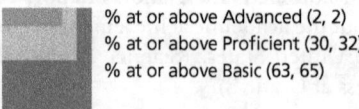

% at or above Advanced (2, 2)
% at or above Proficient (30, 32)
% at or above Basic (63, 65)

Figure 5.2 Achievement-level results in eighth grade NAEP science: 2009 and 2011. *Source:* U.S. Dept. of Education, Institute of Education Sciences, National Center for Education Statistics, National Assessment of Educational Progress (NAEP), 2009 and 2011 Science Assessments.

The Effects of No Child Left Behind and High-Stakes Testing on STEM Education • 55

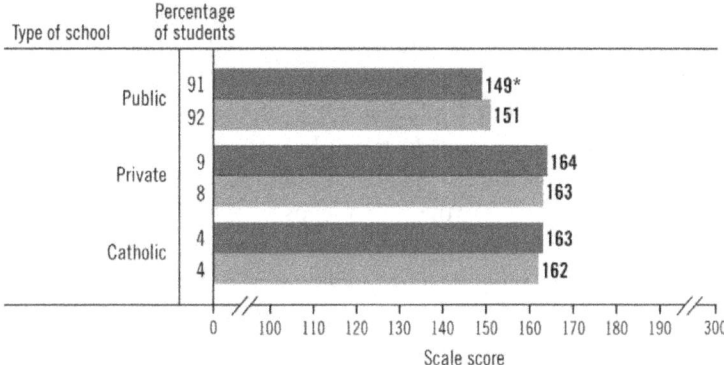

Figure 5.3   Percentage of students and average scores in eighth grade NAEP science, by type of school: 2009 and 2011. *Note:* Private schools include Catholic, other religious and nonsectarian private schools. Detail may not sum to totals because of rounding.

* Significantly different ($p < .05$) from 2011. *Source:* U.S. Dept. of Education, Institute of Education Sciences, National Center for Education Statistics, National Assessment of Educational Progress (NAEP), 2009 and 2011 Science Assessments.

average than non-public school students at both Grades 4 and 8 (on the NAEP; p. 696). While this is not new, their study sought to give an updated analysis of the data comparing public and private school students, to see if current reform movements that tout privatization of public schools is warranted. Some of their findings were surprising.

> While undertaking a broader study of mathematics instruction and equity, we became intrigued by an unexpected finding; when controlling for private school status and student background variables in our statistical models, we saw that mathematics achievement in public schools actually appeared higher than that in private schools. Using a powerful SES (socioeconomic status) variable created for the broader study, we were able to more carefully examine the question of whether the widely assumed "private school effect" is due more to the population of students served than to institutional effectiveness. (p. 697)

Socioeconomic status is divided into four quartiles: low, low-mid, mid-high, and high. These correspond to income levels of families. Their study focused on mathematics.

Upon first look, their results were consistent with much prior research—that the mean of *overall* mathematics achievement of private schools was significantly higher than their public school counterparts. However, since private schools enroll larger numbers of high SES students (public schools enroll about 40% of high SES students, while private schools enroll about 80% high SES students), they wondered if the achievement difference was attributable to SES alone, or if the "private school effect" persisted within each SES group. After controlling for SES levels, Lubienski and Lubienski (2005) found that within each SES quartile, the public school mean is actually higher than that of the corresponding private school mean at both Grades 4 and 8. Specifically, public school fourth grade means were 6 to 7 points higher than private school means within each SES quartile, and eighth grade differences favoring public schools ranged from 1 to 9 points (p. 699). The author's complex statistical models controlled for confounding variables such as race/ethnicity and disability status and still the public school means were higher than private school. This study was an example of "Simpson's Paradox" (or the Yule–Simpson effect)—a phenomenon in statistics where a correlation in different groups reverses when the groups are joined together (Malinas & Bigelow, 2012). Studies such as this may influence the privatization of public schools movement made so popular by No Child Left Behind (2001).

PISA

The National Center for Educational Statistics also conducts international research comparing countries in academic achievement. In the publication "Highlights From PISA 2009: Performance of U.S. 15-year-old students in Reading, Mathematics, and Science Literacy in an International Context" (Fleischman et al., 2010), results were depressing. Scientific literacy is defined in PISA as "the capacity to use scientific knowledge, to identify questions, and to draw evidence-based conclusions in order to understand and help make decisions about the natural world and the changes made to it through human activity (OECD, 2003, p. 15). This speaks to the application and synthesis of knowledge, a higher level of learning than simply knowledge-based facts. According to Yore et al. (2007),

> Scientific and mathematical literacy is intended to promote informed and fuller participation in the public debate about science, technology, mathematics, and environmental issues within the society. Being able to read a newspaper is a common, informal measure of literacy; but making sense of information from many newspapers and other popular print media involves bringing prior, discipline-specific knowledge and literacy strategies to that print to construct understanding and to develop a critical response to the message. (p. 560)

For science literacy as measured by the PISA study, American 15-year-olds scored an average of 502, which placed them 17th in the world, behind such countries as Finland (1), Japan, and Canada (see Figure 5.4).

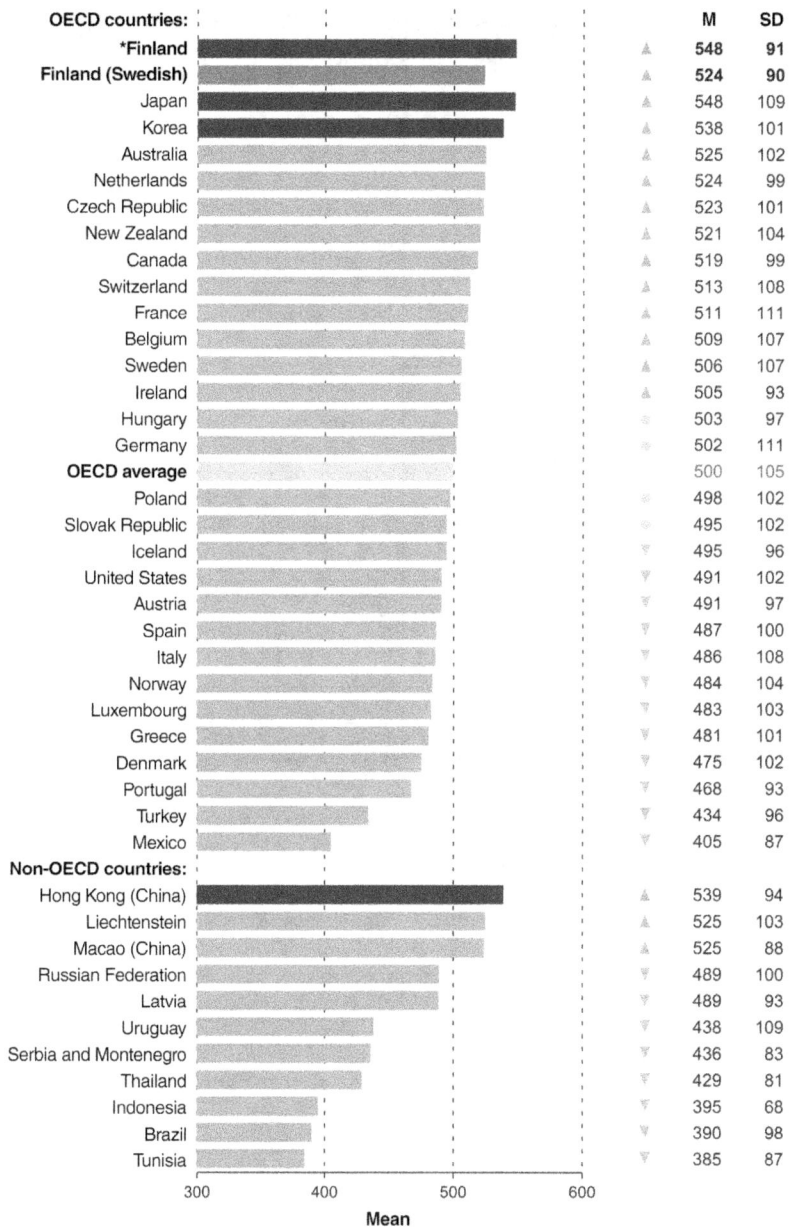

Figure 5.4 Mean performance in scientific literacy. *Source:* Kupari et al. (2004).

TABLE 5.1 Average Scores of 15-Year-Old Students on Mathematics Literacy Scale, by Country: 2009

Mathematics literacy scale		Mathematics literacy scale	
Country	Score	Country	Score
OECD average	496		
OECD countries		**Non-OECD countries**	
Korea, Republic of	546	Shanghai–China	600
Finland	541	Singapore	562
Switzerland	534	Hong Kong–China	555
Japan	529	Chinese Taipei	543
Canada	527	Liechtenstein	536
Netherlands	526	Macao–China	525
New Zealand	519	Latvia	482
Belgium	515	Lithuania	477
Australia	514	Russian Federation	468
Germany	513	Croatia	460
Estonia	512	Dubai–UAE	453
Iceland	507	Serbia, Republic of	442
Denmark	503	Azerbaijan	431
Slovenia	501	Bulgaria	428
Norway	498	Romania	427
France	497	Uruguay	427
Slovak Republic	497	Thailand	419
Austria	496	Trinidad and Tobago	414
Poland	495	Kazakhstan	405
Sweden	494	Montenegro, Republic of	403
Czech Republic	493	Argentina	388
United Kingdom	492	Jordan	387
Hungary	490	Brazil	386
Luxembourg	489	Colombia	381
United States	487	Albania	377
Ireland	487	Tunisia	371
Portugal	487	Indonesia	371

Source: PISA 2009, (p. 18) http://nces.ed.gov/pubs2011/2011004_1.pdf

On April 3, 2013, a story appeared on the CNN ticker: "Former Atlanta Schools Superintendent Reports to Jail in Cheating Scandal" (Gumbrecht et al., 2013). Beverly Hall was one of several school personnel who surrendered to authorities in Atlanta on Tuesday, April 2, 2013. They are being indicted by a grand jury in a cheating scandal that "rocked the district and drew national attention" (Gumbrecht et al., 2013, para. 1). Thirty five educators in all were indicted—including teachers, principals, and testing coordinators. "Charges including racketeering, theft by taking and making false statements about their roles in an alleged plot to falsify students' standardized tests" (Gumbrecht et al., 2013, para. 4). The sad irony was that "Hall was named Superintendent of the Year by the Schools Superintendent Association, which at the time said her 'leadership had turned Atlanta into a model of urban school reform'" (Gumbrecht et al., 2013, para. 5).

Hall had fired principals whose schools did not meet standards, and rewarded those who cheated in order to meet them. A state review had determined that half of Atlanta elementary and middle-schools had cheated on the tests, dating back to 2001 when Hall supposedly started turning around the district by raising test scores. In a statement from American Federation of Teacher's president Randi Weingarten, "Tragically, the Atlanta cheating scandal harmed our children and it crystallizes the unintended consequences of our test-crazed policies" (Gumbrecht et al., 2013, para. 20).

Atlanta is not the only school system in America that has suffered cheating scandals. But Atlanta has been recently in the news for another standardized test cheating scandal. According to Proctor & Lupiani (2024), in 2009, the Atlanta public school system was involved in widespread cheating on the test. Teachers and administrators altered students' test scores on the criterion referenced competency test (CRCT). The cheating involved 44 schools and included 178 educators and 38 principals. They were charged with various crimes, including racketeering, making false statements and influencing witnesses (Proctor & Lupiani, 2024, paras. 18, 19). As long as American schools measure success by high-stakes bubble tests, stories like this are sure to continue.

Obama and Race to the Top

When President Lyndon Johnson enacted the Elementary and Secondary Education Act, or ESEA (1965), public schools across America received federal funding to improve education for the first time in America's history. As a former schoolteacher in Texas, Johnson understood the role of education in fighting poverty and ignorance. ESEA has gone through revisions, including the one called No Child Left Behind. President Barack Obama had stated that NCLB had "created incentives for states to lower their standards; emphasized punishing failure over rewarding success; focused on absolute scores, rather than recognizing growth and progress; and prescribed a pass-fail, one-size-fits-all series of interventions for schools that miss their goals" (The White House, n.d.-b, para. 1). "In March of 2010, the Obama Administration sent Congress a 'Blueprint for Reform of the Elementary and Secondary Education Act,' addressing the issues created by No Child Left Behind while pursuing high standards and closing the achievement gap" (The White House, n.d.-b, para. 2). But because Congress has not acted to reauthorize ESEA, the Administration moved forward in providing states "flexibility within the law—as authorized by provisions in the law itself—to pursue comprehensive plans to improve educational outcomes for all students, close achievement gaps, and improve the quality of teaching" (The White House, n.d.-b, para. 5). To date, 33 states and the District of Columbia have received ESEA flexibility.

On July 4, 2009, President Obama and his secretary of education Arne Duncan created a "contest" whereby school divisions across the country would win points for implementing certain policies, such as adhering to state standards, and for favoring privatization and charter schools. Giving troubled school districts some leeway with NCLB and softening some regulations, his desire was to implement creative alternatives in order to help these districts succeed. However, in his attempt to turn around failing schools, Obama gave in to pressures from those who favored the privatization of American public schooling. According to Diane Ravitch (2010a),

> Duncan set aside $100 billion that Congress had authorized to benefit education in the wake of the economic crisis of 2008. Of the total, Duncan set aside $4.3 billion to promote education reform in what he called the "Race to the Top" fund. To design and manage the Race to the Top, Duncan selected Joanne S. Weiss, a partner and chief operating officer of the NewSchools Venture Fund. Weiss is an education entrepreneur who had previously led several education businesses that sold products and services to schools and colleges. The regulations for the Race to the Top fund excluded any states that limited the number of charter schools or that prohibited a linkage between teacher and principal evaluations and student test scores. (p. 218)

The "contest" called Race to the Top worked as a competition between states to gain federal funds. The states were "scored" with the highest possible score being 500. The criteria were things such as "Great Teachers and Leaders" for 138 total points, with sub-categories being "improving teacher and principal effectiveness based on performance" (58 points), "ensuring equitable distribution of effective teachers and principals" (25 points), "providing high-quality pathways for aspiring teachers and principals" (21 points), "providing effective support to teachers and principals" (20 points), and "improving the effectiveness of teacher and principal preparation programs" (14 points). Other criteria included "state success factors" (125 points), "standards and assessments" (70 points), "general selection criteria" (55 points), "turning around the lowest achieving schools" (50 points), and "data systems to support instruction" (47 points; U.S. Department of Education, 2009, p. 3).

Diane Ravitch had a huge problem with Race to the Top. In her blog from August 1, 2010, she mentioned that President Obama dismisses the criticisms of civil rights leaders who insist that access to federal funding be based on need, not competition (Ravitch, 2010a, para. 2). She mentioned the high-stakes testing craze, the punitive treatment of teachers, grade inflation and cheating, and the push for privatization and charter schools. "President Obama and Secretary Duncan need to stop and think. They are heading in the wrong direction. On their present course, they will end up demoralizing teachers, closing schools that are struggling to improve, dismantling the teaching profession, destabilizing communities, and harming public education" (Ravitch, 2010a, para. 2).

The Privatization of Public Schools

The great American public school system is in extreme danger of being taken over by profit-driven capitalists, whose intentions are not ultimately to raise the level of learning, but to make money and push their agendas. Diane Ravitch, former assistant secretary of education under George Bush Sr., has written an important book concerned with bringing this problem to the attention of the American people. *The Death and Life of the Great American School System: How testing and choice are undermining education* (Ravitch, 2010b), has come out against this system of education reform, believing it to be the privatization of public schooling. What happens when wealthy corporations "help" American public schools? In her chapter entitled "The Billionaire Boys' Club," she points out how rich corporations operate:

> Foundations exist to enable extremely wealthy people to shelter a portion of their capital from taxation, and then to use the money for socially beneficial purposes. Foundations support hospitals, the arts, scientific research, public health, universities, and a host of other worthy philanthropic activities. Foundations themselves may not engage in political advocacy, but they may legally fund organizations that do. They may also support research projects likely to advance the foundation's goals. Education has often been high on their agendas. (Ravitch, 2010b, p. 197)

This sounds wonderful, and indeed, foundations, corporations, and businesses make heroic contributions every day in the American landscape.

However, there will be problems whenever private corporations fund public institutions.

President Obama and his Race to the Top team, instead of listening to the states for their best ideas, presented a list of the administrations' best ideas, few of which are evidence based. Obama told states to adopt as many as possible in order to get the Race to the Top money. According to Ravitch (2010a),

> It's as if a bunch of do-gooders sat together at the NewSchools Venture Fund summit and brainstormed a list of popular reform ideas, and are now going to force them upon the states... Now that the ideas promoted by the venture philanthropies were securely lodged at the highest levels of the Obama administration, policymakers and journalists listened carefully to Bill Gates. In a 2009 interview with Fred Hiatt, editorial page editor of *The Washington Post*, Gates signaled a new direction for his foundation. Hiatt wrote, 'You might call it the Obama-Duncan-Gates-Rhee philosophy of education reform.' Gates said that his foundation intended to help successful charter organizations such as KIPP replicate as quickly as possible and to invest in teacher effectiveness. Gates asserted that there was no connection between teacher quality and such things as experience, certification, advanced degrees, or even deep knowledge of one's subject matter. (p. 219)

The upshot is that test scores are all that matters in the end.

Choice and Charter Schools

The Choice movement began in Minnesota in 1991, when it became the first state to pass legislation that authorized the creation of charter schools. Charter schools thrive in urban districts where academic performance is lowest and the demand for alternatives are greatest (Ravitch, 2010b, p. 125). They can be islands of peace and hope in otherwise miserable neighborhoods.

KIPP is one type of charter school that has gained popularity in recent years. KIPP (knowledge is power program) was started in 1994 by two teachers, David Levin and Michael Feinberg upon completion of their "Teach for America" assignment in Houston. They opened dozens of schools across America, aimed at preparing poor and minority children for college (Ravitch, 2010a, p. 135). The schools are popular and admission depends on a lottery system. There are strict rules, which include; longer days, Saturday classes, and summer school, with students spending 60% more time in school than their non-charter public school peers. Students, parents, and teachers sign contracts (2010a, p. 135). Part of the problem of voicing any downside of such a school is that these schools are really helping improve the quality of life of the students that attend them. There is a dark side to charter schools however.

Have charter schools lived up to their promise? Charter schools in general are no more effective than the average good public school. Ravitch (2010a) says that charter schools run the gamut of success; from poor results to stellar. Most of them are somewhere in between (p. 138, 139). As far as measurable, quantitative results, a scandal was uncovered in 2004. The federal government had tested a sample of American charter schools in 2003, but did not release the findings when it was supposed to in November 2004, when other results were released for states and the nation. They were uncovered on the federal testing agencies website by staff members of the American Federation of Teachers (AFT). Results showed that NAEP (National Assessment of Educational Progress; "Nation's Report Card"), "showed no measurable differences on tests of reading and mathematics between fourth grade students from similar racial/ethnic backgrounds in charter schools and in regular public schools. Among poor students, fourth graders in regular public schools outperformed those in charter schools in both subjects" (Ravitch, 2010a, p. 139).

Overall, charter and public students performed similarly in reading, but public schools students performed better in mathematics. The AFT published its own analysis in August 2004, which raised the question of why the testing data about charters had not been released in a timely manner. The effectiveness of charter schools was especially important, the AFT team argued, because the No Child Left Behind legislation proposed to improve low-performing public schools by turning them into charter schools. If charter schools were no more successful than regular public schools, then the "remedy' made no sense. The AFT leaked its discovery to Diana Jean Schemo, an education reporter at *The New York Times*, whose front-page story stated that "the findings, buried in mountains of data the Education Department released without public announcement, dealt a blow to supporters of the charter school movement, including the Bush administration. The data wars were on" (Ravitch, 2010b, p. 138). The upshot is that charter schools can be wonderful, but they can also be horrible, and those on the lower end of the success scale are not reported.

The lack of reporting mediocrity is not the worst problem in charter schools. It is a shock to some to think that administrators in charter schools fudge their data. Indeed... Diane Ravitch (2010b) says that cheating in charter schools is four times the rate of traditional public schools (p. 155). Why?

> Many ways of gaming the system are not outright illegal, yet they are usually not openly acknowledged. Most principals know that the key to getting

higher test scores is to restrict the admission of low-performing students, because they depress the school's test scores. As choice becomes more common in urban districts, principals of small schools and charter schools—both of which have limited enrollments—may exclude students who are most difficult to educate. They may do it by requiring an interview with parents of applicants, knowing that the parents of the lowest-performing students are not as likely to show up as the parents of more successful students. They may do it by requiring that students write an essay explaining why they want to attend the school. They may ask for letters of recommendation from the students' teachers. They may exclude students with poor attendance records, since poor attendance correlates with poor academic performance. They may limit the number of students they admit who are English-language learners or in need of special education. All such requirements tend to eliminate the lowest performers. Whenever there is competition for admission, canny principals have learned how to spot the kids who will diminish their scores and how to exclude them without appearing to do so. (p. 156)

Among the more successful charters is KIPP. However, the fact that KIPP is so successful is what worries people like Ravitch and myself (Berube). Why? Because *all* public schools should be as successful. We know what works, we know the formula, but children shouldn't have to "win" a lottery in order to attend a good school. What happens to those children whose neighbors win the lottery and gain access to a KIPP school? They are given the opportunity to better their lives. What about those who, through no fault of their own, do not win the lottery and remain back in the neighborhood school? They must continue on with leaking buildings, lack of materials, and teachers so burnt out from lack of support that they barely last a couple of years. Is this fair? Shouldn't the great American school system be the poster child for democracy; without taint from personal money interests?

(KIPP has been funded by Doris and Donald Fisher of "the Gap" line of clothing stores).

Neighborhood School Killer

Is the answer to failing schools privatization and philanthropy? Not if the democratic institution of the American public school must survive. Ravitch (2010b) asserts that these philanthropic foundations, including the Gates foundation, justify their methods by pointing out the low achievement of schools in urban areas, and the success their charter schools have in these districts. But instead of privatization at the expense of public schooling, Ravitch (2010b) offers this instead:

Given the money and power behind charter schools, it seems likely that they are here to stay. If we continue on the present course, with big foundations and the federal government investing heavily in opening more charter schools, the result is predictable. Charter schools in urban centers will enroll the motivated children of the poor, while the regular public schools will become schools of last resort for those who never applied or were rejected. The regular public schools will enroll a disproportionate share of students with learning disabilities and students who are classified as English-language learners; they will enroll the kids from the most troubled home circumstances, the ones with the worst attendance records and the lowest grades and test scores. Indeed, Parker (2013) says that charter schools chronically under-enroll students with special needs. But why not insist that future charters fulfill their original mission, the one Albert Shanker envisioned in 1988? Why shouldn't they be the indispensable institutions that rescue the neediest kids? Why shouldn't they be demonstration centers that show what can be done to help those who can't succeed in a regular school? Why not redesign them to strengthen public education instead of expecting them to compete with and undercut regular public schools? Do we need neighborhood public schools? I believe we do. The neighborhood school is the place where parents meet to share concerns about their children and the place where they learn the practice of democracy. They create a sense of community among strangers. As we lose neighborhood public schools, we lose the one local institution where people congregate and mobilize to solve local problems, where individuals learn to speak up and debate and engage in democratic give-and-take with their neighbors. For more than a century, they have been an essential element of our democratic institution. We abandon them at our peril. (pp. 220, 221)

In Suzi Parker's 2013 blog "TakePart" article *Charter Schools vs. Public: Is One Better Than the Other? New Data Shows Just How Well Kids Are Doing in Many of the Nation's Charter Schools*. Parker makes a case for neighborhood public schools. She quotes Ross Danis, president and CEO of Newark Trust for Education: "So are students really getting *a better education* in charter schools?

"The question, 'Do students get a better education in charter schools?' is complicated," Ross Danis, president and CEO of Newark Trust for Education, told TakePart. He says that a great school is a great school regardless of its classification. "There are effective charters and ineffective charters, and there are effective district schools and ineffective district schools, he said. "As a whole, Newark has a higher percentage of high-performing charters than the entire State of New Jersey (Parker, 2013, para. 6). This is the same argument Diane Ravitch makes. Not all charter schools are winners, just as not all regular public schools are losers.

One of the biggest negative consequences of charter schools are their devastating effects on the neighborhood school. Parker (2013) states,

"Charter schools, regardless of high-achieving academic performance, have a major downside—the death of the neighborhood school."

> School closures in Philadelphia are directly related to the rise of charter school enrollments in the district, as charter schools continue to draw the most motivated families away from their neighborhood schools,' Jerusha Connor, assistant professor of education at Villanova University, told TakePart. (Parker, 2013, para. 13)

Segregation in Charter Schools

Another criticism of charter schools is one that Jonathan Kozol would agree with: the reinstitution of segregation. Kozol interviewed Gary Orfield, formerly of the Harvard Graduate School of Education. According to Kozol (2005),

> Turning to the decade-long debate about school choice, which has sometimes been promoted as "a better way" to break down racial isolation than the more direct route of intentional desegregation, Orfield made an observation with which many of the ardent advocates for choice will not be pleased. "Choice, left to itself," he said, "will increase stratification. Nothing in the way choice systems actually work favors class or racial integration."...As for the current trend toward charter schools, which represent one form of choice, he noted that "most charter schools are more intensely segregated than the average public school, not less...," and he argued firmly against charter schools and other programs of school choice that do not have specific stipulations that will lessen segregation rather than increase it. (pp. 225, 226)

STEM and NCLB

In 2011, congress re-worked NCLB at the request of President Obama and Arne Duncan, then President Obama's secretary of education. In addition to granting waivers to several states to exempt them from certain portions of NCLB, Democratic Iowa Senator Tom Harkin introduced a bill that would revise the act. The part dealing with STEM education included plans to fulfill four goals as follows:

- Improving instruction in STEM subjects through Grade 12
- Improving student engagement in and their access to STEM courses
- Improving the quality of STEM teachers by recruiting and training new teachers as well as improving existing teachers

- Closing the achievement gap between minority and White students and preparing more students for college in STEM subjects. (Koebler, 2011, para. 1)

States receiving grants for STEM would be required to report extensive data, such as STEM teacher evaluations, student achievement in the subjects, rates of access to STEM classes, achievement gaps, and the percentage of students participating in advanced placement or International Baccalaureate STEM courses.

States would be allowed greater leeway to distribute funds earmarked for STEM, as long as they are used to increase access to STEM courses, implement high-quality STEM programs, provide professional development for teachers, or provide technical assistance to schools.

James Brown, executive director of the STEM Education Coalition, a group made up of STEM organizations that worked with Senator Merkley on drafting the legislation, says the bill "covers the gamut of all the different STEM needs."

The bill specifically allows states to use funds to woo engineers, scientists, and other STEM professionals who could potentially be interested in transitioning to a career in teaching and places an emphasis on spending money on STEM programs that have been proven to work.

"It's a relatively small [amount of research], but there's a growing knowledge base of what works in STEM education and what doesn't," he says. "It's about making sure you're spending taxpayer money effectively."

Although the reauthorization of the Elementary and Secondary Education Act has been a controversial, partisan issue for much of the year, Brown says STEM is an issue that has bipartisan support." (Koebler, 2011, paras. 2–7)

Has NCLB Neglected Gifted Students?

If STEM is going to be where the jobs of the future are located, then doing all we can do to support changes in NCLB makes sense. There are some people however, who fault NCLB for the failure of STEM education in America to produce exceptional students, and actually blame it for harming science education. The creators of NCLB had noble intentions—to raise up the achievement of lower-performing students. However, in concentrating only on the low-performing, have we forgotten the gifted? In *Physics Today*, Steven T. Corneliussen (2011) cites an article entitled "The Excellence Gap" by Sol Stern who charges that public schools are focusing on the struggling at the expense of the gifted, and nowhere is this more harmful than in STEM education.

> Stern cites "mounting evidence" of academic decline among the best STEM students. He links this decline to No Child Left Behind, which he charges has "left the door wide open to the corruption of educational standards." He writes: "Though I was among the education writers who enthusiastically supported No Child Left Behind, I should have realized that by focusing almost exclusively on the educationally disadvantaged, yet ignoring the country's future scientists, mathematicians, and engineers, NCLB—despite its framers' best intentions—would damage America's competitiveness. As noble as combating 'the soft bigotry of low expectations' is, America's global standing and economic well-being are more likely to be improved by nurturing a culture of academic excellence and creating programs that support elite education in math and the sciences" (para. 2, 3). Stern blamed the civil rights agenda behind NCLB as the reason everything else was "pushed off the table." Shrinking the racial achievement gap became the number one focus of NCLB, at the expense of everything else, including excellence. Stern also mentioned that districts have "gamed the tests" in order to report rising scores, so as to look good to the feds and the public. He also worries that there are only 100 science and math schools in America, and that only 47,000 are enrolled in them, a very low number. Elite education was never mentioned in NCLB, and Stern declares that "Democrats and Republicans need to reunite and recognize that federal support for elite education—above all, in math and science—is essential for advancing America's economic success." (Corneliussen, 2011, p. 5)

The bottom line is that every school in America should be well-equipped to deliver a high quality STEM instruction. Not just special STEM charters who admit a lucky few with the right lottery number, not just schools in more affluent neighborhoods. Testing is not educating, and accountability is not quality. Pay teachers what they are worth, shrink class size, rely less on standardized tests and allow well-trained teachers to be creative professionals again and many of the problems we face would resolve. If America's educational excellence rests on a lottery system, then how is it different from being born into a caste system in old country Europe hundreds of years ago? Democracy is not about the luck of the draw. The American democratic experiment was supposed to guarantee a shot at equality for all. Choice, accountability, and testing all seem to be the answer to educational problems from people who are not educators. There should be a place at the table for politics in education, but politicians should not be the ones driving the system.

During the Biden administration, public education became a top focus once again. According to PSEA (Pennsylvania State Education Association), the differences between how Biden viewed public education and how Trump viewed it under Betsy DeVoss and her contempt for public schools couldn't be starker. The PSEA states that with education funding for public schools, Biden supports it and Trump supported sending public money to private schools. President Biden supports raises for teachers, including a plan to triple salaries in Title I schools. Trump cut funding for teachers' salaries. President Biden opposed school vouchers which take public money and gives it to private schools, while former President Trump supported vouchers. And maybe the most important difference is that former President Trump hired a woman (Betsy DeVoss) who hated public education and whose brother profited from private schools. President Biden hired a former teacher and principal (Miguel Cardona) who has dedicated his life to American public education and who believes in the mission of public schools. It is clear which president supports American public education (PSEA, 2024).

During the "Trump II" administration, he hired the wife of professional wrestler promoter Linda McMahan as Secretary of Education. What does McMahan know about education? Less than DeVoss did. She is unqualified to lead the department. According to Litvinov (2024), "McMahon is not only unqualified to run the agency, she has spent years pushing policies that would defund and destroy public schools. If this description sounds familiar, it's because McMahon is strikingly similar to Trump's Secretary of Education in his first term, Betsy DeVos" (para. 3). In addition, Litvinov (2024) states: "Rather than working to strengthen public schools, expand learning opportunities for students, and support educators, McMahon's only mission is to eliminate the Department of Education and take away taxpayer dollars from public schools, where 90% of students - and 95% of students with disabilities – learn, and give them to unaccountable and discriminatory private schools," (para. 5). In their wisdom, the administration cut 50% of the Department of Education's staff and programs in the Spring of 2025. Trump would rather us focus on Joe Biden's supposed cognitive decline than what Trump and his administration are doing to our children.

6

What Effective STEM Teaching Looks Like

There is exciting new research showing the way for the next generation of science teachers in America. New techniques with statistically significant achievement outcomes are blazing the path. But when considering good teaching in urban public schools in America, it must be taken into account that we live in a diverse nation, and as such, science needs to be taught using culturally sensitive practices. What types of students inhabit the schools of major urban centers around America? Which cultural and ethnic groups are dominant? How do modern American urban students struggle with language acquisition and assimilation? This chapter will focus on these problems and the new ways to teach science to urban elementary and secondary students in American Public Schools.

Problem-Based Learning

Much has been written lately about the importance of creative teaching in science. The implementation of problem-based learning (PBL) is a new and exciting way to teach science and one that places creative thought at the forefront of teaching and learning. In particular, problem-based learning and project-based inquiry have been emphasized most in fostering creativity in science (Hong & Kang, 2010; Kind & Kind, 2007).

What is PBL? According to Sterling (2007),

> In problem-based instruction, students are presented with a realistic science dilemma, such as the sudden appearance and spread of an unknown disease in a fictional town. Students work collaboratively to research the problem, conduct hands-on activities to learn more about it, incorporate "new" information on the topic (made available through teacher-provided "news flashes"), and eventually make informed recommendations for solving the problem based on their findings. In this way, students are modeling the processes of science and connecting their learning to a real context. (p. 50)

Problem-based learning (Hmelo-Silver, 2004) has been shown to increase student learning by both engaging in finding solutions to real-life problems using science (Sterling & Hargrove, 2012), and prompting them to use higher-order thinking skills. Students who have engaged in problem-based learning experiences such as VISTA have been shown to score more highly on science achievement tests. As Sterling et al. (2010) have shown, not only is problem-based learning sound pedagogy; it is also instrumental in providing marginalized students a learning environment that springboards their learning to close achievement gaps in science, technology, and mathematics (Sterling et al., 2007).

Creativity

No one can argue that creativity is a bad thing, but when considering culturally sensitive teaching and learning, one must examine how different cultures deal with creativity. American creativity might not translate well across cultures. To be creative means that you have a certain, different way of looking at things which is not necessarily the way of the establishment or of the authority structure in charge. Creativity takes a certain amount of rebelliousness and risk-taking and sense of individualism. Certain cultures are more risk-averse and less individualistic than others. These differences are not found just amongst Asian and American students. Hong and Kang (2010) discuss the differences between Korean and American teachers' conceptions of creativity in science teaching:

> While the participants from both South Korea and the United States demonstrated similar trends in their conceptions of creativity and pedagogical ideas, they also revealed some diversity that seemed to originate from socio-cultural differences. The higher proportion of South Korean teachers' consideration of ethicality in judging creativity seems to be related to the Asian cultural emphasis on group goals, which prioritizes consideration of others and contribution to the society (Nisbett, 2003). On the other hand, the higher proportion of the U.S. teachers' emphasis on classroom environmental or emotional support in teaching for creativity seems to be related to the emphasis on individuality, personal goals, or self-aggrandizement in Western culture (Nisbett, 2003). (p. 837)

While the argument that a science teacher's ideas of creativity are a crucial and essential first step for promoting creativity in the science classroom (p. 822), one can see the conflict arising in many urban classrooms. Hong and Kang go on to state that cultural contexts may affect a person's experience of creativity and their ability to manifest it.

> The different emphases of the two cultures also seem to be related to the much lower proportion of Korean teachers' planning for creativity in the classroom. Creativity is inherently a manifestation of individuality, i.e., being different from others. Therefore, teaching for creativity is incompatible with the traditional Asian cultural prejudice against individuality (Kwang & Smith, 2004; Sawyer, 2006). Lim and Plucker (2001), for example, found that Korean people connected social behaviors that implied negative connotations in the Korean culture to creativity. They concluded that this negative social image might inhibit exercising creativity. In the same vein, teachers who honor traditional values might feel reluctant to promote creativity in schools. Therefore, in Asian culture, promoting teaching for creativity seemed to be more challenging and its effect might occur slowly, as it requires changes in values. Although it remains to be seen, the current nationwide promotion of creativity as an educational goal might be effective considering the Asian cultural emphasis on group goals. (p. 838)

No matter what the culture, creative thinking is what separates those who solve global problems in the shrinking world in which we live. Creativity should be encouraged in every American classroom, and with every American multicultural student.

PBL and Creativity

Problem-based learning works in STEM classrooms all across America. It works because it allows students to delve deeply into problems that they themselves solve, not their teachers. The teachers provide scaffolding support and guidance, but the students are the real scientists, technicians, engineers, and mathematicians during these activities. PBL lessons are not meant to take the place of content area learning, but to take it to the next level; to apply what they have learned in the classroom. What does PBL look like?

Here are several examples, all from VISTA—Virginia Initiative for Science Teaching and Achievement at George Mason University, Virginia. These lessons incorporate science, technology, engineering, and mathematics and the students use them together as real world scientists do, not as separate subjects.

Problem-Based Learning Template

Theme	Science topic
Problem	Real scientific problem with multiple solutions stated as a question that will be solved over time
Student Roles	Authentic scientist roles for students
Scenario	Real situation and setting that is interesting and plausible
Resources	Identify and evaluate likely places students will seek information to solve the problem—internet, books, expert
Culminating Project/Assessment	
	Develop a final project that poses a solution
Safety	Identify safety issues that might arise as students gather information

(VISTA 2012)

The template is provided in order to offer a framework for each individual PBL lesson. Here are some examples of such lessons from the science education faculty academy held at George Mason University, May 21–25, 2012 in Fairfax Virginia:

Problem-Solving Cycle for Teachers

Problem Solving Cycle

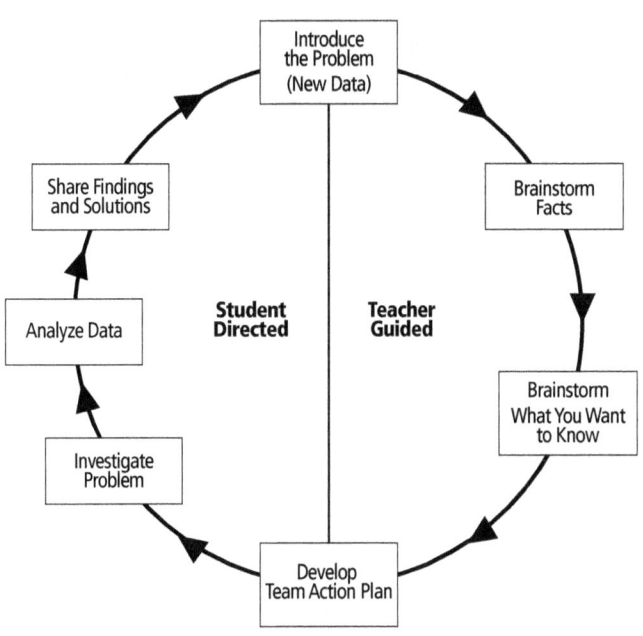

Sample Health-Related Problem and Scenario Designed by Teachers

HEALTH: PROBLEM-BASED LEARNING TEMPLATE

Theme	Medical Mysteries
Problem	What disease is causing the outbreak and how will you prevent it from spreading?
Student Roles	Team of researchers—epidemiologists
Scenario	Several people in Masonville have become ill. A team of researchers has been asked to assess the situation, make recommendations to prevent

	the spread of infection, and possibly cure the disease. You are that team!!!
Resources	Internet, textbook, encyclopedia, dictionary, and community resources such as health professionals
Culminating Assessment	PowerPoint presentation including the proposed cause for the disease and method of prevention, plus a 3D model of the bacteria/virus causing the disease

SAMPLE PBL SCENARIO FOR MEDICAL MYSTERIES DESIGNED BY TEACHERS AND SHARED WITH STUDENTS

Newsflash! Outbreak Feared!

Doctors across Masonville are reporting more and more patients with symptoms similar to Mae Fairfax's symptoms. Not only are patients experiencing a high fever, vomiting, and sluggishness, the infected individuals are experiencing other symptoms as well.

Our on-the-street reporter had the opportunity to interview Mr. Bach Teria. However, Mr. Teria was very confused and often forgot what he was saying: "Every time I...Hmmm...Well...Every time I look at the Sun...I look... I...Hmmm...It hurts my eyes...What was I saying? Hey! Who are you?" During the interview Mr. Teria constantly scratched at the rash on his skin.

Although many doctors declined interviews, Dr. Inc U. Bashion has offered us this glimpse of hope: "You can be assured that our best scientists are working on this problem as we speak."

SAMPLE TEAM ACTION PLAN SCAFFOLDING COMPLETED BY STUDENTS

(Question brainstorming over four activity sessions during Medical Mysteries)

Action Plan		
What do you know?	Where or how will you find out?	Who is responsible?
Note: First complete this column as a whole class on the board, projector, or flipchart so all students	Science textbook Computer encyclopedia	Sally and Keisha Omar and Trin

can contribute and see the list as the class develops it. When this action plan chart is distributed, the students copy the list here. On successive days when new information and symptoms are learned, they are added here.	Internet	Sally and Keisha
	Internet	Omar and Trin
	Internet	All
	Internet	Omar and Trin
	Dr. Jackson—neighbor	Keisha
	School nurse	Sally
	Internet	All—difference diseases

SAMPLE LETTER CREATED BY TEACHERS PROVIDES CLUES FOR THE MEDICAL MYSTERY STUDENTS ARE SOLVING

Dr. Jan Ross
Microbiologist
Thompson Hall, Room 222

George Mason University
11222 Microbe Drive
Masonville, VA 20202

To: Dean M. Jordan

From: Dr. Jan Ross

Dear Dean Jordan,

In response to your request, we have analyzed the blood samples of the 114 patients from Masonville who have exhibited the symptoms from this mysterious illness. We prepared slides and examined them under our microscopes at the lab. We did find various microorganisms (bacteria) but nothing unusual. The bacteria seen in the samples are found in healthy individuals as well. As you know, we no longer have an electron microscope in the lab to determine if it is something other than bacteria causing the illness. We have sent the blood samples out to the CDC Medical Facility Lab in Reston, Virginia for further analysis and investigation. The CDC Medical Facility has one of the best electron microscopes in the nation. There, they will be able to determine the exact cause of the illness. The lab results should be in by the end of the week.

Sincerely,
Dr. Jan Ross

Sample Earth Science-Related Problem and Scenario Created by Teachers

EARTH SCIENCE: PROBLEM-BASED LEARNING TEMPLATE

Theme	Weather Tamers
Problem	How do you construct a natural disaster-proof city?
Student Roles	Team of researchers at Federal Emergency Management Association
Community Partner Roles	Civil engineers, meteorologists, college-based research scientists in the earth sciences
Scenario Focus	As "junior weather tamers" your task is to design and construct a model of a city that could serve as a prototype disaster-resistant model for all areas of the United States. This city should be able to withstand natural disasters in any given area no matter the location so that the people living in that area would remain safe.
Alternative Scenario	A storm is approaching—News releases are given from President _____ and weather forecasters that describe the changing weather events
Resources	Internet, textbook, encyclopedia, dictionary, civil engineers, meteorologists, college-based research scientists in the earth sciences
Culminating Assessment	Test model cities

SAMPLE CHALLENGES CREATED BY THE TEACHER FOR STUDENTS TO CONFRONT

President _____ sends the "Junior Weather Tamers" on missions around the United States:

Natural Disaster	Location	Challenging Conditions
Hurricanes	Miami, Florida	Rising water due to storm surge and run off, high winds, rain
Tornadoes	Oklahoma City, Oklahoma	High winds, hail, rain, flying debris
"Earthquake Weather" (science misconception)	San Francisco, California	Intense heat, no breeze, drought, seismic waves
Mystery Natural Disaster (final test)	????????	Teacher selects type and strength of natural disaster

SAMPLE SAFETY PLAN CREATED BY STUDENTS

Safety Plan for Conducting Experiments for Weather Tamers

What is our question?	What data do we need?	What is our procedure?	What are the risks to students and teacher(s)?	How do we prevent safety mishaps?	How do we handle safety mishaps?
How does the model of our city withstand high winds?	Numbers of structures damaged and description of damage to each structure	1. Place city model in designated location for test. 2. Group members stand in designated location behind the source of wind. 3. If selected to operate blow dryer, hold blow dryer at agreed upon height and direction. 4. Turn on blow dryers as instructed by teacher(s). 5. Record data as it happens if not holding a blow dryer. 6. Turn off blow dryers as instructed by teacher(s). 7. Place blow dryer in designated location. 8. Record data of final outcome.	Damage to eyes from flying debris from structures; electric shock from touching metal prongs, touching a wet blow dryer and/or cord, or using a blow dryer with an improperly grounded electric outlet	Wear goggles at all times; one group tests at a time under teacher supervision; instruct all group members to stay at one end of model; blow hair dryers in one direction away from where group members are standing; inspect cord; ensure that electric outlet is grounded and appropriate extension cord is used, if needed; plug and unplug cord by holding non-metal part of plug; keep hair dryer and cord dry at all times.	Inform teacher(s) at once if group member struck by object; do not touch wet hair dryer or cord and step back.

VISTA, 2012; Science Education Faculty Academy, Fairfax, VA.

What Every Teacher Should Know About Physics but Is Afraid to Ask

We have a dilemma; if you love... I mean really love science, you are probably teaching it at the high school, maybe middle school level, where you teach nothing but science all day long. The problem is that by middle school, most children have given up on science, or have had a succession of awful teachers and have lost interest in something they think is dry and boring. Those elementary school teachers who have to teach every subject each and every day are terrified of science; they hate it and many don't even teach it every day. When I was getting my master's in teaching degree, my project was to uncover the awful truth that there are many elementary school teachers who ignore and neglect science weekly just because they themselves don't like it. But it is just those elementary school years when each and every child in America should be falling in love with science for life. We need to get the elementary school teachers of America on board with science.

The notion that science is hard, boring, and impossible to understand is a myth. All one has to do to shatter this myth is to read a book by Brian Greene, physicist professor at Columbia University and star of the PBS documentary "The Elegant Universe" (B. Greene, 2012, http://www.pbs.org/wgbh/nova/physics/elegant-universe.html). Dr. Greene writes these books for regular people. He has sections in the back of his books for those who want to delve deeper into mathematics, but the average Joe can understand the most complicated concepts in the universe by reading books such as these. Why? Because they are written in a conceptual way, with no complicated math or special skills needed for understanding. Why don't most people think that they can understand relativity or string theory? Because they don't *believe* that they can. Once a person realizes that they can understand topics in physics that were once thought to be the domain of Einstein-like scientists, it is tremendously empowering. It can change a person's belief about him or herself and what they are capable of. It can literally change a life. But first, the teachers need to learn it.

Why am I picking on physics? Because it is the most intimidating of the science fields to non-scientists. Maybe because of Albert Einstein and his $E = mc^2$ (a very simple notion by the way); maybe because America is locked into the ridiculous "nerd" notion that brainiacs are not cool. Maybe for a lot of reasons. But some of the leading "personalities" in the world (famous scientists) are in the field of physics, including Brian Greene; Neil deGrasse Tyson, director of the Hayden Planetarium in New York City (who also happens to be African-American), and Michio Kaku, physicist at City College, CUNY. These and other "rock star" scientists are gathering a loyal layperson following—regular folks who read their books and enjoy their humor and charm. And they are getting hooked on science.

Research has shown that teacher self-efficacy (confidence and feelings of competence) *precede* good teaching; in other words, before a teacher tackles a content area, he or she has to feel relatively secure in the belief (important word here... *belief*) that they can actually do a good job of it. In my book *The X Factor: Personality Traits of Exceptional Science Teachers* (Berube, 2010), I present such research on teacher self-efficacy:

> Bleicher conducted a study in 2004, whereby he measured science teacher self-efficacy and outcome expectancy in pre-service elementary school teachers. The instrument he used was the STEBI-B, or the Science Teaching Efficacy Belief Instrument-Pre-ervice. The STEBI-B measures two constructs based on Bandura's notion of self-efficacy; outcome expectation (the notion that people will perform an action if they believe it will have a favorable result), and self-efficacy (they are confident that they can perform that action successfully.
>
> Research shows that teachers who lack confidence in what they are teaching are less likely to teach science (Ramey-Gassert & Shroyer, 1992; Bleicher, 2004). Science is a subject unlike any other in that the nature of science is one of forward movement. In other words, science content is constantly changing, and this can be intimidating to a new teacher, who is trying to juggle so many things at once. Tosun (2000) conducted a study to measure the effects of previous science education courses on science self-efficacy in pre-service teachers. "The results suggested that prior science course experience and achievement have little impact on the belief systems of future teachers of science (para. 1)." To be more precise: "It was clear that the discipline-integrated methods course played some role in increasing the science teaching self-efficacy of the pre-service teachers, although their outcome expectancy remained unchanged. The precise influence of the methods course cannot be determined since there were other variables that may have influenced the beliefs of the students" (para. 19).
>
> Tosun also states that "The finding that there were no significant differences between the low group students and the high group students on both the self-efficacy and outcome expectancy scales prior to exposure to the methods course was consistent with Bandura's social cognitive theory... behavior is shaped by an interaction of behavior, cognitive, and other personal factors, and environment events. Science content knowledge may play a role, but it is not the primary factor that determines the success of a teacher... this should not be taken as to totally dismiss the role of science content knowledge but, instead, to point to the notion that teacher education programs must be sure to address teacher efficacy beliefs" (para. 23). What this means is that feeling incompetent in a certain science topic is only *part* of why a teacher may have low self-efficacy. *Beliefs* of whether they can master the content seem to be *just as important* a factor in teacher success.

> Isn't that what we strive to impart to our students... the notion that they can do something if they believe they can? (pp. 13, 14)

The research is clear, that the belief that one can master a subject is needed before mastery can even occur. I mention this because of all of the science topics, as mentioned earlier, physics seems to be the most menacing to those not familiar with it. The job for elementary teachers therefore, is to learn as much as they can from sources such as those mentioned (see Appendix). It's also a job for colleges and universities of teacher education—physics must be included in general elementary education teacher preparation programs in order to graduate elementary school teachers who feel confident with the subject.

An example I gave in *The X Factor* is about gravity. Think about what you learned about gravity—that it causes objects to fall to earth. But *why?*

> In 2008, I wrote an article entitled "Atoms, Strings, Apples and Gravity: What the Average American Science Teacher Does Not Teach," where I discussed the lack of sufficient content knowledge by most elementary and middle school science teachers. Especially when it comes to physics and topics like the notion of gravity. As mentioned earlier, biology seems to be the area that gives teachers the most comfort, with physics the most discomfort. Do most teachers think that physics is too difficult for them to learn? We remember learning about gravity as children. We were told that it is a force of attraction. As I mentioned earlier, we all think we know what gravity is, but can you actually explain *why* it works?
>
> But what exactly causes gravity? How do bodies pull on each other? The Newtonian theory of gravity is based on a simple model, one in which bodies attract each other with a force proportional to a quantity called their mass and inversely proportional to the square of the distance between them. This model predicts the motions of the sun, moon, and planets to a high degree of accuracy (Hawking, 1988). But while it describes certain components of gravity, it does not explain why objects are attracted to each other. Scientists have known what creates the force we know as gravity for more than one hundred years; however, most lay people do not know it. Einstein said space was not empty but interwoven with time, creating a "fabric" he called *space-time*. Events do not occur in space independent of time. The concept of space-time is difficult to visualize because humans are accustomed to two dimensions, such as diagrams of the surface of the earth (longitude and latitude). And yet, to understand the concept of gravity, we must accept that time and space are not separate entities but are intertwined, forming a fabric affected by the planets and bodies in it. This is known as the theory of relativity (Hawking, 1988).
>
> When Einstein made this discovery, it changed all of history, not just science. He discovered that gravity has two components, acceleration and mass. Ein-

stein said the pressing force we identify as gravity is merely accelerated motion, much like what we feel in an elevator that is going up. We feel heavier heading toward the penthouse and lighter descending to the lobby. Greene (2004) states, "Einstein realized that gravity and accelerated motion are two sides of the same coin" (p. 65). The feeling of acceleration is indistinguishable from gravity. "Since gravity and acceleration are equivalent, if you feel gravity's influence, you must be accelerating" (p. 67). That is, a person is moving even when sitting still on earth as the earth is hurtling through space at 68,000 miles per hour, therefore, one feels the effects of gravity. Although this explains much of the feeling of gravity, there is yet another aspect that explains the apparent attraction between objects. Einstein found that mass bends and warps the space around it. Photos of sunbeams during total solar eclipses in 1919 and 1922 proved that light bent around the earth as it traveled past. Much like a bowling ball resting on a trampoline, the earth and all matter bend the space around them, accounting for the planets' orbits (see Figure 6.1).

The larger the mass, the tighter the orbit of the planet. That is, just as a larger bowling ball will result in a deeper warp in the trampoline than a smaller bowling ball, a larger planet will make a larger, deeper warp in space-time than a smaller planet, thereby attracting smaller objects (lesser planets) toward itself. When an object becomes trapped near the larger planet, it results in an orbit around the larger planet (Berube, 2008b).

This correct concept of gravity is not taught in most science education classes by science education professors, so how can we expect elementary school

The Effects of Mass on the Fabric of Space–Time

Figure 6.1 This two-dimensional representation of four dimensional space-time seeks to show how the mass of planets and other objects in space, actually bend and warp the space around them, thereby contributing to orbits and gravity.
Source: http://www.pbs.org/wnet/hawking/strange/html/gravity.htm

teachers to correctly teach the concept of gravity? This is just one example of why so many pre-service teachers are scared of science, and unnecessarily so. It isn't properly taught to pre-service teachers who are planning to teach science, so in turn, when they have their own science classrooms, they don't teach it properly to the children. (Berube, 2010, pp. 16–18)

When I (Berube) taught sixth and seventh grade science, I decided one year to try to teach concepts such as these to my students. I remember a certain sixth grade science class where I was teaching about the fabric of space-time (you can find writing on this in almost every book in the Appendix) and how time slows down as you reach the speed of light (relativity). They thought that time was a constant in the universe until I told them that time is an illusion and can change if space is bent. I described to them how we normally experience three dimensions here on earth; north/south, east/west, and up/down. But there is a fourth dimension—time. We are traveling through time as we are also traveling through the other dimensions. If you are in a parked car on the street...you are not traveling north/south, east/west, or up/down. But you *are* traveling through time. The energy given to the dimension of time is 100%. However, if you speed off at 60 miles an hour north/south...some of that energy previously devoted to time is *now given to a direction*, so time actually slows down for you. Why can't we detect this on earth? Because we are traveling too slowly. If we were to approach the speed of light, 186,000 miles per second...time would stop. We would be giving so much energy to the dimension of direction, none would be left over for the time dimension. We would literally be in a timeless dimension. This is amazing stuff, it's been proven and the average student in American schools doesn't know this. The average *teacher* in American schools doesn't know this. It's been known to humanity for over 100 years, yet we consider it too difficult to learn. Kids love this...they love to talk about time travel, space adventures, and "what if" you could travel back and change the past? They love to write papers using their imaginations on this topic. It's a lost opportunity to get kids hooked on science when the adults don't know how to teach it.

7

Educational Malpractice and the Mishandling of STEM Education Pre- and Post-Pandemic

Sueanne E. McKinney
Kala Burrell-Craft

Much attention and spirited debates worldwide (both uprightness and fabricated) continue to focus on the recovery and revitalization of society because of the effects of COVID-19. We continue to be plagued by the compounded problems and complexities ignited by race politics, the municipal public, and the political agenda. Amid these multiple pandemics, education (next to healthcare and the murdering of Black and Brown bodies) has taken the greatest hit. In education, our children are still impacted by poverty, the lack of access to high quality curricula, diverse teachers/leaders, stimulating STEM education, and the Whitewashing of American history.

As both researchers and practitioners, we are often befuddled when classroom discussions by seasoned and preservice teachers and leaders leave out the impact poverty has on our students. We often hear from teachers and leaders that "kids are kids" and "children are children"; however, this could not be further from the truth. As Haberman (1995) stated:

> The difficulties facing students and teachers in the largest urban districts in the United States are different from those in smaller districts. In urban schools, students are generally poor, educationally challenged, limited in language, or handicapped in other ways. Home conditions for many students may not include a parent, and the community's support for learning is neutral at best. Increasing occurrences of school violence, drug abuse, displaying weapons in school, and misbehaving reflect the social problems occurring outside the schoolhouse. When such conditions are part of a student's life, teaching and is significantly affected. (p. ix)

Further, the Global Alliance (2021) expands on Haberman's (1995) argument that "All kids are not just kids":

> Child poverty and the violation of children's rights are increasingly an urban phenomenon. An estimated billion people live in overcrowded, inadequate housing without basic services or secure tenure. More than a third are children and adolescents, living in conditions that challenge their rights, well-being, and long-term prospects. Yet urban children have surprisingly few global champions and can often be overlooked in more general agendas. (p. 3)

While we do not subscribe to the deficient way of thinking about students who live in urban areas, we do feel it is important to quote the dire and desolate literature that is easily accessible and implicates Black and Brown students as being almost hopeless. However, to push back on this deficient way of thinking we want to point out that urban areas exist because of systemic racial policies, politics, disenfranchisement of a people, and disinvestment in Black and Brown communities.

The system is functioning exactly the way it was designed and according to Global Alliance (2023), it is expected that the comparative percentage of impoverished children and adolescents in urban areas are anticipated to persist and continue to remain at a high proportion for decades to come. While school districts attempt to acquire population percentages in all schools by the use of "Federal Cards," presently there are no national channels of identifying and categorizing the most vulnerable, under resourced, and poorest urban children in need (Friedman & Daniello, 2010; Global Alliance, 2021; Hill-Jackson & Stafford, 2017), let alone creating a plan that would disrupt this system of inequity.

Challenges Pre and Post Pandemic

Systems of inequities existed long before the pandemic in urban areas. Systems like state and national assessments, little or no honors/gifted/advanced placement courses, lack of quality daycare/before and after-school programs, unfair discipline practices, and the criminalization of Black boys are a few of the ways lack of access and unequitable educational practices have harmed urban communities of color. Childhood trauma is a significant public health concern that can evoke irreversible damage to children, families, and society. The exact estimates of its prevalence are difficult to obtain and study due to underreporting, inadequate surveillance systems, and definitional inconsistencies (Saunders & Adams, 2014), but numerous studies have concluded that childhood trauma is widespread (Copeland et al., 2007; Fantuzzo et al., 2007). Urban areas have been identified as a specific geographic area in which childhood trauma reports are underreported and underrepresented. According to Goldfeld and colleagues (2015), urban areas pose five unique domains related to child development: physical environment, social environment, socioeconomic conditions, services, and governance. Physical environment refers to items such as parks, transportation, housing, and other built environment conditions (Lavin et al., 2006; Prado-Galbarro et al., 2021). The social environment consists of factors such as crime, trust, and safety, and socioeconomic conditions include poverty, employment, and access to education. Services include institutional resources such as schools, headstart/daycare centers, and healthcare facilities. Governance often looks at citizen engagement, leadership, and social coordination (Prado-Galbarro et al., 2021; Goldfeld et al., 2015). Some impacts of racialized systems in urban America include, but are not limited to:

- untenable living conditions (poor quality and over crowded conditions);
- young children who are left unmonitored at home (working parent);
- engaging in risk taking behaviors (Early sexual contact, alcohol);
- neighborhood violence (theft and violent crimes);
- lack of healthy food, and food in general (food desert);
- lack of 2-parent household (disproportionate incarceration of Black males);
- illegal drugs with easy access (Snowfall series, Idris et al., 2018);
- witnessed a murder, shooting or gang violence;
- chronic absenteeism;
- limited access to basic services and amenities;
- shame and social stigma, anxiety;

- economic exclusion and opportunities (disinvestment in communities of color);
- trauma;
- inexperienced teachers of those with provisional licenses; and
- face eviction (Global Insights, 2023; Haberman, 1995, 2005; Hill-Jackson & Stafford, 2017; Idris et al., 2018).

Overall, close to 900,000 nonfatal incidents are committed yearly at schools, and near 1.3 million reports of alcohol, drugs, weapons, and/or violence on the school grounds yearly (Roberts et al., 2015). Take for example, in January 2023, a teacher in Newport News, Virginia, was shot and seriously injured by a 6-year-old child who later boasted about it by stating, "I shot that bitch dead" (Todd, 2023, para. 8). This 6-year-old child is a prime example of a dysfunctional system. First, a 6-year-old having access to a firearm is problematic. Other problematic functions of this example include the narrative spun by the media stating the 6-year-old has a "history of violence" and the media quoting the child saying "I shot that bitch dead"—these villainize the child and skews the public's opinion of what happened and what led up to the incident. It takes the narrative off the school and the teacher and places it squarely on the child and their family. The teacher is suing for $40 million dollars. Trauma can cause people to question and re-evaluate their commitments to goals, values, roles, and beliefs. Experiencing traumatic events at an early age might make specific goals seem less obtainable and challenge one's beliefs about the world. Worry and anxiety about the inability to resolve identity issues are known as identity distress (Berman et al., 2004), which has been linked to trauma (Ertorer, 2014; Merrill et al., 2016). Trauma can cause identity delay, identity threat, and identity loss (Waterman, 2020). Just as trauma affects identity, identity can affect how trauma is perceived, interpreted, and experienced. Brenner (2017) states our integration of emotion and intellect, our basic awareness of our emotional state, and the feeling of security as an individual are disrupted when we experience developmental trauma. Early trauma shifts the trajectory of brain development because an environment influenced by fear and neglect causes different adaptations of brain circuitry than one of safety, security, and love. The COVID-19 virus exasperated an already critical situation, but it also brought the disparities of urban communities back into mainstream discussion. For example, poor areas in and around New York City experienced death rates 15 times higher than other poor areas (Global Alliance, 2021). The Global Alliance (2021) concluded:

> The COVID-19 pandemic, although its effects are not concentrated on children, sheds a harsh light on the inequities facing the urban poor, exposing,

and exacerbating their disproportionate risk. Along with the absence of supportive healthcare services and uncertainties of getting food, the issues of high density, inadequate water supplies, poor sanitation, drainage, and waste collection, and the lack of secure, adequate housing make social distancing and self-quarantine impractical, and foster the rapid spread of the virus. (p. 13)

The Impact of the Pandemic on STEM Education

An estimated 1.6 billion students' learning was disrupted, globally, by the pandemic. We went from the abrupt closing of schools to virtual learning, then back to in-person learning. It is not surprising that long term trend data revealed extreme debilities and declines in both mathematics and reading achievement scores among American students during COVID-19's first 2 years (National Assessment of Educational Progress, 2022). The "Nation's Report Card" reported that on average, math scores revealed the first 5-point statistically significant drop in scores since the early 1970s. Likewise, reading showed the first 4-point significant regression since 1980–1984. In due course, this achievement data in both content areas revealed an estimated loss and limitation of approximately 2 decades of school progress (National Assessment of Educational Progress, 2022). According to Mervosh and Wu (2022), the results from the first test results since the beginning of COVID-19, mathematics scores declined in every state for eighth graders. Only 26% of them were identified as proficient, a weakening of nearly 34% compared to 2019. Additionally, fourth graders declined in 41 states with only 36% determined to be proficient in mathematics. This was down from 41% previously.

The National Assessment of Educational Progress, a nonpartisan data center, made note that this decline in scores was experienced most intensely among those students who had previously struggled at the highest rate before the pandemic occurred. When examining racial and ethnic groups, all groups experienced statistically significant declines in reading and math, leading the achievement score gap to increase from 25 to 32 points (National Assessment of Educational Progress, 2022).

Science education in many districts was simply derailed during the pandemic as schools focused on mathematics and reading. Based on an analysis of data from AmeriSpeak, over a third of high school students stated they were "moderately" or "extremely" worried over the incompletion of their STEM courses. This survey was nationally representative and included about 2,000 students ages 13–17 (Sparks, 2021). In many states science support was limited, and lacked project-based, hands-on activities that would ignite student interest in STEM careers.

Key data collected by The Nations Report Card (2022) is reported in Table 7.1 and based on the National Assessment of Educational Progress (NAEP). The chart is interactive, and provides scores in mathematics, reading, writing, and science for Grades 4, 8, and 12. It can be found at https://www.nationsreportcard.gov/profiles/stateprofile?chort=1&sub=MAT&sj=&sfj=NP&st=MN&year=2022R3 and provides you with a more in-depth understanding of the progress of each state.

TABLE 7.1 The Nations Report Card (2022)

Area	Average Score (0–500)		Achievement Level Percentages	
	Score	Difference From National Public (NP)	At or Above Basic	At or Above Proficient
Wyoming	243	8	84	44
Wisconsin	240	5	79	43
West Virginia	226	–9	67	23
Washington	235	#	74	35
Virginia	236	1	75	38
Vermont	234	–1	74	34
Utah	240	5	78	42
Texas	239	4	78	38
Tennessee	236	1	76	36
South Dakota	239	4	80	40
South Carolina	234	–1	74	34
Rhode Island	234	–1	74	34
Puerto Rico	178	–57	10	#
Pennsylvania	238	3	76	40
Oregon	228	–7	66	29
Oklahoma	229	–5	71	27
Ohio	238	3	76	40
North Dakota	240	5	81	40
North Carolina	236	1	75	35
New York	227	–8	66	28
New Mexico	221	–14	60	19
New Jersey	239	4	77	39
New Hampshire	239	5	80	40
Nevada	229	–6	69	28

(continued)

TABLE 7.1 The Nations Report Card (2022) (continued)

Area	Average Score (0–500)		Achievement Level Percentages	
	Score	Difference From National Public (NP)	At or Above Basic	At or Above Proficient
Nebraska	242	7	80	43
National public	235	†	74	35
Montana	239	4	80	38
Missouri	232	–2	72	34
Mississippi	234	–1	74	32
Minnesota	239	4	78	41
Michigan	232	–3	71	32
Massachusetts	242	7	79	43
Maryland	229	–6	65	31
Maine	233	–2	75	32
Louisiana	229	–6	69	27
Kentucky	234	–1	75	33
Kansas	235	#	75	35
Iowa	240	5	80	40
Indiana	239	4	78	40
Illinois	237	2	76	38
Idaho	236	1	76	36
Hawaii	237	2	77	37
Georgia	235	#	75	34
Florida	241	6	81	41
DoDEA	250	15	92	51
District of Columbia	223	–12	57	24
Delaware	226	–9	64	26
Connecticut	236	1	74	37
Colorado	236	1	75	36
California	230	–4	67	30
Arkansas	228	–7	69	28
Arizona	232	–3	70	32
Alaska	226	–9	65	28
Alabama	230	–5	71	27

▲ Significantly higher than National public
◆ Not significantly different from National public
▼ Significantly lower than National public

Federal officials govern the NAEP assessment and educators view this assessment as rigorous and more demanding than traditional state level tests. It is estimated that the sample size was approximately 450,000 fourth and eighth graders housed in more than 100 schools. Miguel Cardona, U.S. Secretary of Education, stated:

> The results released today from the National Assessment of Educational Progress are appalling, unacceptable, and a reminder of the impact that this pandemic has had on our learners. The data also represent a call to action for the important work we must do now for our students—especially those who have suffered the most during the pandemic. (Misuraca & Hall, 2022, para. 2)

Cardona further remarked to CNN'S Brianna Keilar,

> If this is not a wake-up call for us to double down our efforts and improve education, even before it was—before the pandemic, then I don't know what is" during an appearance on "New Day" Monday. (CNN, October, 2022, 0:45)

Undoubtedly politics played a significant role when governors made the decision to close and reopen schools. Sean Reardon, a professor of education at Stanford, reported that comparing states is difficult. Often, they are based along party lines. For example, in Texas, a Republican state, schools were opened earlier than most, reading scores held constant, but math scores declined. California (a Democratic state) demonstrated caution in reopening their schools and achievement scores fell slightly less than the national average but was similar to the scores in Florida (a Republican state)—which served as the front runner in the early opening of schools. Virus transmission rates were also a factor in the opening and closing of schools, which was often left out of the political discussions (Esquivel, 2022). A clear analysis of scores needs to be conducted before conclusions are made regarding school openings and closings, and the role they played.

Revitalizing the Spark for STEM Education for Urban Learners

Promoting resilience, positive mindsets, and instilling hope within urban students are a few first steps that teachers can undertake in promoting STEM education now that schools have reopened (Bashant, 2020; Haberman, 2005). Haberman (2008) refers to this as "Gentle Teaching in a Violent Society," and he and prominent culturally responsive educators such as Ladson-Billings (1995) and Delpit (1995) suggests the following:

- Ignite student interest in the material; don't just "cover" the content.
- Emphasize student effort and potential.
- Hear and use ideas presented by students.
- Model positive interactions.
- Show respect for student opinions.
- Encourage students to express their feelings.
- Recognize the special gifts that each child brings to the classroom and allow opportunities for them to showcase their talents.
- Promote community and collaboration.

Bashant (2020) and Burrell-Craft (2022) also add to this list by highlighting additional strategies and the conversation of identity development:

- Intrinsic motivation
- Understanding student trauma
- Implement restorative practices.

The COVID-19 pandemic brought to the forefront the inequalities in education especially for the country's most vulnerable urban students. The research indicates that achievement levels had a sharper drop, leaving them further behind their White peers, and widening the opportunity gap that has existed since the systems of oppression were created. It will be a daunting task to assist urban, high-poverty children to climb to proficiency. Doing less is "educational malpractice" for our marginalized children. However, with a clear plan of action supported by the government, culturally responsive leaders and teachers, and a dismantling of the current system, rebounding is a possible and achievable goal, but it must be a priority!

8

Conclusion

The Future of American STEM Education

In 2024, STEM classrooms in American public schools look a little differently than they did just a few short years ago; especially since the COVID-19 pandemic. Most recently, the phenomenon of AI (artificial intelligence) has taken over teacher, school board, and university professor debates as to how to incorporate AI into school—if at all. How can you tell if your student wrote his or her paper if AI can do it for them? Are there appropriate uses for AI in American public-school classrooms? It is definitely part of the STEM world and also part of the working world they will be hired into upon graduation from high school or college. What are the moral and ethical questions surrounding AI—in a world where deep-fake videos can make it appear that someone you know in the public sphere is saying or doing something they in fact did not say or do? We are on a precipice of danger but also great possibilities. Can American public education handle this in the current anti-intellectual atmosphere?

If STEM is the key to the global economy of tomorrow, then what does the future hold for American public-school students entering the workforce? What does the future hold for American global economic dominance, if we are not ready to embrace the intellectual curiosity and scientific mindset that is necessary for success in STEM fields? If Americans are not willing to let scientific facts and discoveries inform their belief systems, but instead filter out facts to fit belief systems—as in the case of members of the Flat Earth Society who believe that the earth is flat and that the NASA moon program was a hoax or in those that believe that the earth is 6,000 years old instead of 4.5 billion—then what does that say about the fitness of America to maintain its leadership status in the world?

In 2006, The Neanderthal Genome Project formed as a collaboration of scientists coordinated by the Max Planck Institute for Evolutionary Anthropology to map out the genome of the Neanderthal—an extinct subspecies of Homo sapiens, related to early humans. From fossil evidence, Neanderthals and modern humans diverged from a common ancestor in Europe as early as 600,000–350,000 years ago (Bischoff et al., 2003). Some researchers suggest that modern humans and Neanderthals split off into different evolutionary branches 700,000 years ago (Zimmer, 2013). The project published their results in the May 2010 journal *Science* detailing an initial draft of the Neanderthal genome based on the analysis of 4 billion base pairs of Neanderthal DNA. The study determined that some mixture of genes occurred between Neanderthals and anatomically modern humans and presented evidence that elements of their genome remain in that of non-African modern humans (Green et al., 2010).

David Reich, a geneticist at Harvard Medical School, was part of this project. His findings revolutionized the world of evolutionary biology. Reich's work on Neanderthal and modern human inbreeding refuted the purely "out of Africa" model of human evolution, because African Americans hold no Neanderthal DNA in their cells. Reich found that once in a while (not a common occurrence), Neanderthals and humans had sex that produced children.

> Reich and his colleagues had no choice but to conclude that Neanderthals had mated with humans. They estimated that the DNA of living Asians and Europeans was (on average) 2.5% Neanderthal. They had to reject a pure version of the out-of-Africa model. Instead, their model was closer to out-of-Africa-and-get-to-know-some-Neanderthals-very-well. The patterns Reich and his colleagues identified can help narrow down when and where the interbreeding took place. Since Africans do not carry Neanderthal DNA, it would appear Neanderthals bred only with the ancestors of Europeans and Asians. One possibility is that when humans emerged out of Africa some 50,000 or more years ago, they encountered Neanderthals in the Near East. (Zimmer, 2013, p. 4)

What this means is that scientists can take a sample of a living person's DNA and tell if they have any Neanderthal DNA in their cells. Billions of living humans do, including those of White European and Asian descent.

On May 22, 2013, the discovery of a well-preserved 39,000 year woolly mammoth by an expedition of the Russian Geographical Society—that had been frozen in Siberian soil—caused a world-wide sensation. The finding was incredible not only because mammoths have been extinct for thousands of years, but because red blood flowed out after the mammoth had been hit with a pickaxe. The blood was saved in tubes for further scientific examination. The finding of the mammoth with liquid blood raised the question of a real-life Jurassic Park scenario, where scientists could possibly clone an actual woolly mammoth. The possibility is breathtaking...could this actually happen? Modern science has the pieces of the puzzle, the rest is just a matter of time (Lupanov, 2013).

It is getting more and more difficult to deny the age of the planet, or the existence of evolutionary processes in living things. Global climate change is ignored and denied by powerful leaders of industry who profit from the denials. The problem is that many people do deny it, even in the face of real evidence. Nowhere else on Earth is there such a problem with scientific evidence. Other countries that practice religious belief systems also take science seriously. While there is no doubt that the rights of free Americans include the right to believe in any way one chooses, there are real consequences for these choices. If the disrespect for science and intellectual thought in America continues on its current path, then within one or two generations, we can expect to be a mediocre country inhabited by mediocre people whose belief systems precipitate a slide backwards not seen since ancient Rome. The STEM jobs will be completely occupied by foreign intellectuals and scientists, schoolchildren will lose the wonder and excitement that only scientific discovery can bring, and the dreamers and visionaries will live in other lands.

According to Engler (2012),

> For America, improving achievement in science, technology, engineering, and math will go a long way to ensuring that our country can compete globally, create jobs, and achieve the levels of economic growth that will buttress Americans' standard of living and social safety net. High-quality STEM education represents an opportunity that students, workers, educators, and business must seize if we are to keep the country strong. (para. 12)

The problem, according to Engler, remains the lack of interest in STEM careers:

> But despite the lucrative potential, many young people are reluctant to enter into fields that require a background in science, technology, engineering, or mathematics. In a recent study by the Lemelson–MIT invention index, which gauges innovation aptitude among young adults, 60 percent of young adults (ages 16 to 25) named at least one factor that prevented them from pursuing further education or work in the STEM fields. Thirty-four percent said they don't know much about the fields, a third said they were too challenging, and 28 percent said they were not well-prepared at school to seek further education in these areas. (Engler, 2012, para. 6)

American schools are not properly preparing youngsters for careers in STEM. Since schools function within societies, we can hold American culture partly responsible for this dilemma. Whenever it is cool to be stupid, science suffers.

This is a problem—for young people and for our country. We need STEM-related talent to compete globally, and we will need it even more in the future. It is not a matter of choice; for the United States to remain the global innovation leader, we must make the most of all of the potential STEM talent this country has to offer. Morella (2013a) asked Robert Curbeam, an African-American astronaut, what he saw ahead in terms of future space travel and research in the article "Making STEM Matter for the Next Generation of Astronauts and Engineers." Curbeam stated,

> At the end of the day, we're going to need a lot of very, very smart and informed and knowledgeable people in the next generation to help us continue to push that forward. Although we sit here and we're very, very worried about the short term—how do we get people that are qualified to do the jobs we have now?—we also have to think a generation away: How are we going to make sure that we have the people to do that work in 2030, 2040, 2050? ("What do you see ahead...," para. 1)

Morella (2013b) also discusses how as many as 60% of high school students who begin in STEM are giving up on STEM fields by graduation time.

Is there nothing to ignite young people's imaginations anymore concerning science? Neil de Grasse-Tyson—director of the Hayden Planetarium and star of "NOVA Science Now"—wishes there was. de Grasse-Tyson hosts "Star Talk," a radio show where he interviews scientists and offers solutions to scientific problems facing America today. de Grasse-Tyson thinks that American children have nothing to shoot for or dream about concerning space exploration anymore. No vision for the space program. No children dreaming of becoming astronauts anymore. No American society cheering for our scientists and rooting for their successes. Does the world-wide political climate have anything to do with this current lack of enthusiasm? Is there better science during times of international strife than during peacetime? In the Season 4, Episode 2 podcast (de Grasse-Tyson, 2013), de Grasse-Tyson (2013) speaks with Professor John Logsdon—former director of the Space Policy Institute at George Washington University. de Grasse-Tyson mentions that NASA was created in a different climate—in a cold-war climate.

So how do geo-politics matter to the mission statement of NASA? During Obama's second inauguration speech, the president said we have a "new Sputnik moment" in America. de Grasse-Tyson (2013) has a problem with his speech. The problem with that speech, according to de Grasse-Tyson, is that it offers no new visions for the future, only technology that we already have, such as light-rail or high-speed internet. The real Sputnik moment included expanding the boundaries of human possibility; doing something we had *never* done before, or even barely imagined. Every president tries to craft a vision statement concerning NASA, but politics uses NASA as a political ping-pong ball, depending on the political leanings of the president. However, the greatest resolve actually occurs when we compete with other countries, not during periods of great cooperation.

The geo-political culture of competition, and the impetus to out-do other countries, seems to be the best fertile backdrop for scientific research. de Grasse-Tyson (2013) does believe however, that during peace, we can and should produce good science. How much importance we place on space programs however, is telling. The equivalent of the entire budget of NASA is spent every 4 days by defense (de Grasse-Tyson, 2013). What matters to Americans is where we spend our money, and what *makes* us money. The military-industrial complex generates billions of dollars in revenue for the country. We are invested in discord, not peace. War is big business, and many times, the scientific endeavors that are invested in and funded by the federal government are those that can contribute to this aim; including technological advances which aid the war effort, including nuclear capabilities. Indeed, those countries that hold the most power are those with nuclear weapon technology. This capability tends to create loud, arrogant, and boisterous countries that are more apt to start and engage in wars than those without it.

At present, the United States spends almost $1 trillion annually on defense-related purposes (Higgs, 2007). America spends 23% of its total budget on the military, while it spends 3% on education (usgovernmentspending.com, 2013). This translates to education receiving $67.7 billion, and defense receiving $666.2 billion (United States Office of Management and Budget, 2012). Motivations aside, even if scientific learning in America will always be related to defense, we are still at a loss to produce home-grown STEM experts in numbers that would ensure global dominance in these fields.

The U.S. Department of Education (n.d.) has posted a page entitled "Science, Technology, Engineering, and Math: Education for Global Leadership," which acknowledges the challenges of STEM education in America, and outlines some solutions. The Obama administration has projected that the number of STEM jobs will steadily climb during the next decade and that we need to properly prepare high school and college graduates in order to prevent losing these jobs to foreign interests (see Figure 8.1).

According to the U.S. Department of Education (n.d.), only 16% of American high school seniors are currently proficient in mathematics and interested in a STEM career ("The Need"). In order to remedy this, President Obama has called on the nation to properly train 100,000 STEM teachers over the next decade. He has asked colleges and universities to graduate 1 million students with STEM majors. These things will happen, only if Hispanics, African-Americans, and women are fully participating in STEM. The Obama administration has promised to secure funding for this, and to invest in K–12 instruction, higher education, graduate fellowships, and experiential out-of-the-classroom learning (U.S. Department of Education, n.d., "The Goals").

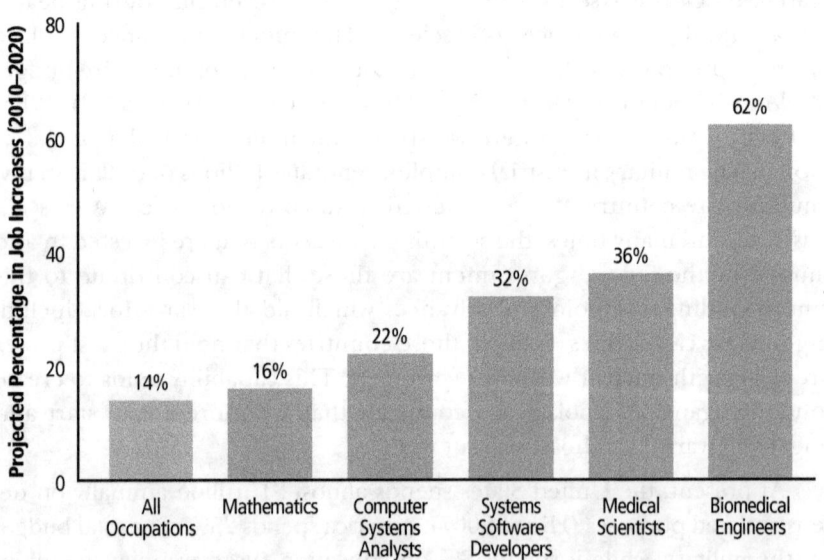

Figure 8.1 Projected Percentage Increases in STEM Jobs (2010–2020). U.S. Department of Education website: Science, Technology, Engineering and Math: Education for Global Leadership. *Source:* http://www.ed.gov/stem, July 11, 2013.

When President Biden was in office, there was a press release on the Whitehouse website entitled "President Biden Announces New Actions to Advance Racial and Educational Equity on 70th Anniversary of Brown v. Board of Education" (The White House, n.d.-a) which states that the strength of the American economy is inextricably linked to the stated strength of America's school system. To this end, the White House offered these approaches to solving these problems:

- New Magnet School Grants: The Department of Education's Magnet Schools Assistance Program (MSAP) will invest $20 million in new awards for school districts in Arkansas, Colorado, Florida, Kentucky, Louisiana, North Carolina, and Texas to establish magnet programs designed to further desegregate public schools by attracting students from different social, economic, ethnic, and racial backgrounds. The president's 2025 budget request includes $139 million for MSAP and $10 million to continue investments in the Fostering Diverse Schools program.
- Establishing a new technical assistance center to help states and school districts provide more equitable and adequate approaches to school funding. The U.S. Department of Education announced a new Technical Assistance Center on Fiscal Equity as part of the Comprehensive Centers Program. The Center on Fiscal Equity will provide capacity-building services to support states and school districts build equitable and adequate resource allocation strategies, improve the quality and transparency of fiscal data, and prioritize supports for students and communities with the greatest need.
- New Data on Equal Access to Math and Science Courses. The Department of Education Office for Civil Rights is releasing a new Civil Rights Data Collection report highlighting students' access to and enrollment in mathematics, science, and computer science courses and academic programs, drawing from information in the 2020–21 Civil Rights Data Collection (CRDC). The report reflects stark continuing racial inequities in access to math, science, and computer science courses for students in high schools with high concentrations of Black and Latino students.
- Preserving African American History. To further advance the President's Executive Order on Promoting the Arts, the Humanities, and Museum and Library Services, the Administration is launching an interagency process to develop new actions by the Federal Government to preserve African American history—including preserving historic sites, protecting and increasing access to literature, and ensuring the public, including students, has continuing access to resources. This effort will bolster African American history and culture as integral, indelible parts of American history. (The White House, n.d.-a, paras. 5–8)

Solutions

It would be difficult to not offer as a solution a whole change of political administration but that is my first real solution. Not until Donald Trump and

TABLE 8.1 Diversity in Ivy League Schools, 2023

School	Women	Non-White Students	Black Students	Students in Historically Underrepresented Groups
Brown University	51%	62%	8%	20%
Columbia University	49%	68%	7%	23%
Cornell University	54%	67%	7%	23%
Dartmouth College	49%	52%	6%	17%
Harvard University	52%	65%	9%	21%
University of Pennsylvania	55%	67%	8%	19%
Princeton University	50%	63%	8%	18%
Yale University	51%	65%	8%	24%

Source: Nam, 2024

his second administration get booted out of office will there be any hope for America in general, let alone public education. Until that happens we must fight back with all our might against the current autocratic movement among American Republicans who wish to drag us back into the Dark Ages. With midterms a year away we must demand our rights to our elected officials, including the right for children to learn in non-biased public schools; free from religious dogma and dumbed-down textbooks. American politicians in power know the real value of education—that is exactly why they want to harm it. They have graduated from Harvard, and Yale, and Princeton. They know the power that resides there and the power it bestows to its graduates. According to Nam (2024), Ivy League schools are among the most diverse in the Nation, with Columbia University leading the pack. Is it hard to figure out why the power elite don't want diversity in Harvard and Columbia among others? And why Donald Trump is so hell bent on punishing them right now? (see Table 8.1).

In the opinion of the author, there are several things American schools must do in order to raise the level of STEM education:

- Insist on abandoning the ridiculous anti-intellectual climate currently popular in most of America. This includes stressing the importance of school and intellectual activities.
- Related to anti-intellectualism: creating a mindset that allows belief in God and belief in science. This is and always has been a false choice. Until the average American accepts as fact scientific concepts such as evolution and climate change, there is no hope.

- Financial resources: where a person or country spends money is a good indicator of what they care about. War is necessary from time to time, but if constant on-going wars are funded at the expense of the public school system, then the decline of America will be swift.
- Respect for the teaching profession: this includes strengthening and expanding teacher unions, including those in Southern states. The urban myth of teachers as lazy malcontents that are hard to fire and caring only for their pensions has to cease. The teacher-bashing that goes on in the United States is breathtaking, leading to fewer young people choosing teaching as a profession. Increasing respect naturally means much higher pay for teachers. In Finland where the world's best schools are located, teachers are some of the most respected and highest paid workers in the country. If we pay teachers what they are worth, more talent will be pulled from other fields such as the pure sciences and engineering, which pay much higher salaries. This will also help solve the problem of science incompetence among elementary school teachers and ensure that American children develop a love for science from a very early age.
- Quit focusing on a few charter schools and instead concentrate on strengthening each and every neighborhood school in terms of STEM education and classes. A great education should not rely on winning a lottery or how much money your parents make. If this is the case, we may as well go back to the old-country caste system that drove many of our ancestors to leave for America.
- With the focus of the federal government on true school reform, we will become less reliant on private individuals and corporations for school funding. Can you imagine if the American military was funded in this way? The thought is frightening.
- Push for integration of schools once again. All students learn better when they are in school together. Not only that, but it improves neighborhoods and the lives of students on both ends of the spectrum.
- Less reliance on one shot high-stakes tests as measures of accountability, and more on higher level critical thinking skills via teaching pedagogy such as problem-based learning and student centered learning. Testing is boring, true learning is exhilarating.
- Colleges and universities with teacher education programs must maintain high standards for programs, stressing a balance between content and pedagogy.

As mentioned earlier in this book, whenever school districts benefit from the generosity of corporations such as Apple, Microsoft, or Bill Gates, there are strings attached. This is a delicate balancing act, because even as the schools that are helped by these business leaders will most definitely improve their physical surroundings and technological capabilities, they may also be forced to incorporate those teaching and learning tools and programs prescribed by these corporations, whether they are educational best-practices or not. Educators that conduct educational research may be pushed aside by business people and politicians with the power and leverage to enforce their will on the public school system with programs that may be faddish or popular, but meaningless. It may be very tempting to sell your soul to the charter school movement, or to the notion of competition and privatization. While these choices exist, they should *never* replace the great democratic and free American public school system.

The ultimate danger in doing so is in a return to the permanent caste and class system that our forebears left their homes for during the great immigration of past centuries. The danger is in a future school system where the affluent middle and upper middle class receive the best education, granted to them not by some noble superiority, but by money. You should not have to buy a good education. This is not to say that private schools in this country are bad; on the contrary, some of the best schools in America are those that charge tuition. Yet... the education afforded to those in the lower socioeconomic rungs in society should still be of a high enough quality so that the children graduating from these free public institutions have a chance to rise in status so that maybe one day they themselves will have the luxury of choice as to where to send their children. The argument of choice is sometimes warped; it's not that choice is a bad thing, it's that so few actually have real choice!

Parents Rights?

Finally, the new "parents right movement" that has taken hold in many public schools across the country is a movement on the surface meant to give parents some control over their children's education. This is in itself not a bad thing. Parents have been looking to have more control for decades. The problem with the current version of this movement is that many parents are looking to narrow curriculum, which doesn't just affect their child, but the whole classroom of children. From banning books to re-writing history to forcing religious articles in public school classrooms, they claim to do it for "freedom." Whose freedom? I will finish this book with an op ed I wrote in the *The Virginian-Pilot* newspaper—published in 2023.

OPINION: VIRGINIA MUST ENSURE PUBLIC SCHOOLS ARE WELCOMING TO EVERYONE.

I agree with Darcie Cimarusti's Dec. 26 column, "Beware of the so-called parents' rights movement." Yes, parents are vital, but politically motivated groups confuse re-writing history and book banning as "parents' rights."

My husband Maurice Berube, a retired professor of educational leadership at Old Dominion University, was active in the community control movement in New York City in the 1960s (featured in the "Eyes on the Prize" documentary). While at the Institute of Community Studies at Queens College, he co-authored a seminal book, "Confrontation at Ocean Hill-Brownsville." As an education aide for Mayor John Lindsey, he also worked for the great labor union leader Al Shanker as managing editor of the United Teacher, a publication of the American Federation of Teachers.

The community control movement was an experiment for three minority school districts in which parents would make up the school board and have a hand in hiring and firing teachers and curriculum choices. Ocean Hill-Brownsville, Brooklyn, was a minority district and the movement was a reaction to discrimination.

While a noble idea, it blew up into a major confrontation, with strikes from teachers who rebelled against being fired or reassigned with no cause. Public schools shut down for three months in 1968 until the mayor called off the experiment.

While ultimately not successful, it gave parents some power in what their children learned and started awareness of the historically inaccurate textbooks and curriculum. It originated from voicelessness and "whitewashing" of history.

The current "parents' rights" movement has none of that history of struggle or oppression, but as members of the majority culture, whose story has always been told. Public schools are a vehicle for democracy, meaning that anyone should be able to attend and graduate prepared for the American dream. Are there people invested in the failure of public education? Private money is trying to push agendas in American public education. Public schools by definition should have no ideology or agenda other than educating our children.

Bullying teachers and school boards is popular today. This is outrageous and would be loudly condemned a generation ago. Disrespecting teachers? Unheard of. Parents and teachers were a team. Do these parents wonder why their children are misbehaving at school? Why should these kids respect their elders or their teachers when mommy or daddy don't?

Virginia teachers have strict guidelines as to what to teach during the year, easily located on the Virginia Department of Education's website under the Standards of Learning for each grade. There is no "critical race theory"—a theory taught to law school students. CRT is a fear tactic used by politicians for political reasons. Virginia SOLs (Standards of Learning) include lessons on slavery. When I was in school, pre-SOL, we learned about slavery as well, and no one seemed to care. Worried about a handful of library books? Have you seen your kid's internet search history? Anger over library books is misplaced. Being well-read is a positive.

I am a champion of public schools because it is the most American institution we have. A good neighborhood school is vital for the health of a community. Unfortunately, there is a movement to privatize public schools instead of investing in them.

Parents have choices in child rearing, but the public school needs to be a place for everyone. Education is a public service. College is different; even public colleges charge tuition. But free public K–12 schools are vital for democracy.

Many Americans' ancestors were educated in America's free public schools. Poverty stricken, they were fleeing oppression or hunger or death. American public schools were here for them so you can be where you are today, no matter your political party or religion. As Cimarusti said, policies that respect and affirm all students should be the work of good public schools.

Clair Berube, PhD, *is an assistant professor of education at Virginia Wesleyan University in Virginia Beach and author of "The Investments: An American Conspiracy."*

(Berube, 2023)

Sometimes I ponder the notion of what mindset a person would have to have in order to leave everything they know and love for an unknown land. It must have been terrifying. They were willing to endure whatever was necessary in order to secure for themselves and their families that "American dream" of upward social mobility. Americans are not locked into a lifestyle from birth, destined forever to rise only as high as those that came before them. In the old country, if your father was a peasant, then so were you. Americans are different. Why? Because of the Great American public school system.

References

Abbate-Vaughn, J., Frechon, O., & Wright, B. (2010). Accomplished urban teaching. *Theory Into Practice, 49*(3), 185–192. https://doi.org/10.1080/00405841.2010.487752

Adelman, C. (1998). *Women and men of the engineering path: A model for analyses of undergraduate careers.* U.S. Department of Education, Office of Education Research and Improvement. https://eric.ed.gov/?id=ED419696

American Association for the Advancement of Science. (1990). *Science for all Americans—Project 2061.* Oxford University Press.

American Association of University Women Educational Foundation. (1995). *How schools shortchange girls: The AAUW report: A study of major findings on girls and education.* Marlowe & Co.

American Journeys. (n.d.). *Historical highlights.* http://www.americanjourneys.org/highlights.asp

Armenta, T., & Lane, K. (2010). Tennessee to Texas: Tracing the evolution controversy in public education. *The Clearing House, 83*(3), 76–79. https://eric.ed.gov/?id=EJ878813

Aronson, J., Steele, C. M., Salinas, M. F., & Lustina, M. J. (1998). The effects of stereotype threat on the standardized test performance of college students (adjusted for group differences on SAT). In J. Aronson (Ed.), *Readings about the social animal* (8th ed.; pp. 400–412). Worth.

Atwater, M., Wiggins, J., & Gardner, C. (1995). A study of urban middle school students with high and low attitudes toward science. *Journal of Research in Science Teaching, 32,* 665–677. https://doi.org/10.1002/tea.3660320610

Bajak, A., Machado, T., & Wihhey, J. (2020, May 26). *The 2020 census and Title I funding for schools: Interactive maps to localize your state's stakes.* The Journalist's

Resource. https://journalistsresource.org/economics/2020-census-title-i-maps/

Baron, E., Rusnak, T., Brookhart, S., Burrett, K., & Whordley, D. (1992, March 20–24). *Collaborative urban education: Characteristics of successful urban teachers* [Paper presentation]. AASA Convention, San Diego, CA.

Bashant, J. (2020). *Building a trauma-informed, compassionate classroom: Strategies and activities to reduce challenging behaviors, improve learning outcomes, and increase student engagement.* PESI Publishing & Media.

Basso, R. (2012, March 2). *How STEM jobs are leading our future and why you should care.* Basso on Business Blog. http://www.openforum.com/articles/how-stem-jobs-are-leading-our-future-and-why-you-should-care

Bennen, S. (2000). Inherit the wind monkeys with the Scopes trial on teaching evolution. *Education Digest, 66*(2), 60–63.

Berkman, M. B., Pacheco, J. S., & Plutzer, E. (2008). Evolution and creationism in America's classrooms: A national portrait. *PLoBiology, 6,* 920–924. https://doi.org/10.1371/journal.pbio.0060124

Berman, S. L., Montgomery, M. J., & Kurtines, W. M. (2004). The development and validation of a measure of identity distress. *Identity: An International Journal of Theory and Research, 4*(1), 1–8. https://doi.org/10.1207/S1532706XID0401_1

Berry, R. Q., III. (2003). Mathematics standards, cultural styles, and learning preferences: The plight and the promise of African American students. *The Clearing House, 76*(5), 244–249. https://doi.org/10.1080/00098650309602013

Berube, C. T. (2004). Are standards preventing good teaching? *Clearing House, 77*(6), 264.

Berube, C. T. (2008a). Atoms, strings, apples and gravity—What the average American science teacher does not teach. *The Clearing House, 81*(5), 223–226. https://doi.org/10.3200/TCHS.81.5.223-226

Berube, C. T. (2008b). *The unfinished quest—The plight of progressive science education in the age of standards.* Information Age Publishing.

Berube, C. T. (2009, May 25). Learning about God from fossils. *The Chronicle of Higher Education* [Letters to the editor]. https://www.chronicle.com/article/learning-about-god-from-fossils/

Berube, C. T. (2010). *The x factor: Personality traits of exceptional science teachers.* Information Age Publishing.

Berube, C. (2023, June 23). Opinion: Virginia must ensure public schools are welcoming to everyone. *The Virginian-Pilot.* https://www.pilotonline.com/2023/01/07/opinion-virginia-must-ensure-public-schools-are-welcoming-to-everyone/

Berube, M. R. (2000). *Eminent educators: Studies in intellectual influence.* Greenwood Press.

Bilen-Grene, C., Froelich, K., & Jacobson, S., (2008, June 8–10). *The prevalence of women in academic leadership positions, and potential impact on prevalence of women in the professorial ranks* [Paper presentation]. WEPAN 2008

National Conference: Gateway to Diversity: Getting Results Through Strategic Communications, St. Louis, MO.

Bischoff, J. L., Shamp, D. D., Arumburu, A., Arsuaga, J. L., Carbonell, E., & de Castro, J. M. B. (2003). The Sima de los Huesos Hominids date to beyond U/Th equilibrium (>350 kyr) and perhaps to 400–500 kyr: New radiometric dates. *Journal of Archaeological Science 30*(30), 275–280. https://doi.org/10.1006/jasc.2002.0834

Bleicher, R. (2010). Revisiting the STEBI-B: Measuring self-efficacy in preservice elementary teachers. *School Science & Mathematics, 104*(8), 383–391.

Bouchrika, I. (2024). *What is a Title I school? A guide to funding benefits & requirements in 2024.* Research.com. Research.com/education/what-is-a-title-1-school

Boule, II, J., (2003). Washington: Engineer and engineer advocate. *Past in Review,* Jan–March, 2003 (pp. 51–55). https://apps.dtic.mil/sti/pdfs/ADA596623.pdf. Accessed May 28, 2025.

Bransford, J. D., Brown, A. L., & Cocking, R. R. (Eds.). (1999). *How people learn: Brain, mind, experience, and school.* National Academy Press.

Brenner, G. (2017, July 1). *6 ways that a rough childhood can affect adult relationships.* https://www.psychologytoday.com/us/blog/experimentations/201707/6-ways-rough-childhood-can-affect-adult-relationships

Brickhouse, N. W., & Potter, J. T. (2001). Young women's scientific identity formation in an urban context. *Journal of Research in Science Teaching, 38,* 965–980. https://doi.org/10.1002/tea.1041

Burrell-Craft, K. (2022). Psychological lynching: An examination of educational trauma and identity development. *Journal of Trauma Studies in Education, 1*(3), 135–155. https://doi.org/10.32674/jtse.v1i3.5055

Campbell, R., Dempsey, A., Margolin, E., Mathewson, G., & Reichbach, E. (1983, January 30–February 2). *Basic competencies and characteristics of the successful urban teacher* [Paper presentation]. Annual Meeting of the Association of Teacher Educators, Orlando, Florida.

Capraro, R. M., & Slough, S. W. (2013). *Why PBL? Why STEM? Why now? An introduction to STEM Project-Based Learning.* In R. M. Capraro, M. M. Capraro, & J. R. Morgan (Eds.), *STEM project-based learning* (pp. 1–5). Sense Publishers. https://doi.org/10.1007/978-94-6209-143-6_1

Carnegie Science Center. (2012, May 29). Careers of the future. *Pittsburgh Magazine.* http://www.pittsburghmagazine.com/Pittsburgh-Magazine/June-2012/STEM-Careers-of-the-Future-Pittsburgh/

Carter, P. L., & Welner, K. (2013). *Closing the opportunity gap: What America must do to give every child an even chance.* Oxford University Press.

Castro, A. (2009, March 7). *Texans forge compromise on evolution.* MSNBC. https://www.nbcnews.com/id/wbna29902944

Chang, K. (2012, September 25). Bias persists for women of science, a study finds. *The New York Times: Science Times,* p. D1, D6. https://www.nytimes.com/2012/09/25/science/bias-persists-against-women-of-science-a-study-says.html

Chesler, N. C., & Chesler, M. A. (2002). Gender-informed mentoring strategies for women engineering scholars: On establishing a caring community. *Journal of Engineering Education, 91*, 49–55. https://doi.org/10.1002/j.2168-9830.2002.tb00672.x

Clauston, D. & Gerstel, N., (2002). Caring for our young: Childcare in Europe and the United States. *Contexts, Sage Journal, 1*(4), 4–72.

Clawson, X, & Gerstel, X. (2002). *U.S. childcare seriously lags behind that of Europe.* NewsWise, https://www.newswise.com/articles/us-childcare-seriously-lags-behind-that-of-europe

Clewell, B., Campbell, P., & Perlman, L. (2007). *Good schools in poor neighborhoods: Defying demographics, achieving success.* The Urban Institute.

CNN. (October, 2022). *New Day broadcast* [Televison episode]. https://x.com/brikeilarcnn/status/1584512700801253378?mx=2

Copeland, W. E., Keeler, G., Angold, A., & Costello, E. J. (2007). Traumatic events and posttraumatic stress in childhood. *Archives of General Psychiatry, 64*(5), 577–584. http://doi.org/10.1001/archpsyc.64.5.577

Corneliussen, S. (2011, December 14). Does "No Child Left Behind" force the scanting of gifted STEM students? *Physics Today.* https://doi.org/10.1063/PT.4.0221

CQ Press. (2005). No Child Left Behind: Is the law improving student performance? *The CQ Researcher, 15*(20), 469–492. https://bpb-us-e1.wpmucdn.com/sites.suffolk.edu/dist/7/135/files/2010/01/cqresearch-nclb.pdf

Darnell, A., & Sherkat, D. (1997). The impact of protestant fundamentalism on educational attainment. *American Sociological Review, 62*(2), 306–315. https://doi.org/10.2307/2657306

de Grasse-Tyson, N. (2013, May, 19), *Space chronicles (Part 2)* [Podcast]. http://www.startalkradio.net/show/space-chronicles-part-2/

Deiss, H. (2023). *STS-135: The final voyage, NASA multimedia.* https://www.nasa.gov/missions/space-shuttle/sts-135/sts-135-the-final-voyage/

Delpit, L. (1995). *Other people's children: Cultural conflict in the classroom.* New Press.

Diamond, M. (1999, January 8). *Why Einstein's brain?* [Lecture delivered at Doe Library]. https://web.archive.org/web/20170504015541/http://education.jhu.edu/PD/newhorizons/Neurosciences/articles/einstein/index.html

Dunbar, D., & Kennersley, R. (2011). Mentoring female administrators toward leadership success. *Delta Gamma Kappa Bulletin, 77*(3), 17–24.

Ebner, J., & Herring, L. (2002). *U.S. childcare seriously lags behind that of Europe.* American Sociological Association.

Ehlers, V. (2010, September 28). *Reflecting on STEM education.* The Hill. http://thehill.com/special-reports/education-september-2010/121473-reflecting-on-stem-education

Eisenkraft, A. (2003). Expanding the 5e model: A proposed 7e model emphasizes "transfer of learning" and the importance of eliciting prior understanding. *National Science Teaching Association, 70*(6), 56–59.

Ellison, C. G., & Musick, M. (1995). Conservative protestantism and public opinion toward science. *Review of Religious Research, 36,* 245–262. https://doi.org/10.2307/3511533

Engler, J. (2012, June 15). *STEM education is the key to U.S.'s economic future.* U.S. News and World Report. https://www.usnews.com/opinion/articles/2012/06/15/stem-education-is-the-key-to-the-uss-economic-future

Erikson, E. H. (1950). *Childhood and society.* W. W. Norton.

Ertorer, S. E. (2014). Managing identity in the face of resettlement. *Identity: An International Journal of Theory and Research, 14*(4), 268–285. https://doi.org/10.1080/15283488.2014.944695

Esquivel, P. (2022). *Test scores across US reveal "heartbreaking" pandemic declines, with math hit hard.* https://www.latimes.com/california/story/2022-10-23/test-scores-united-states-pandemic-setbacks-math

Fantuzzo, J., Bulotsky-Shearer, R., McDermott, P. A., McWayne, C., Frye, D., & Perlman, S. (2007). Investigation of dimensions of social-emotional classroom behavior and school readiness for low-income urban preschool children. *School Psychology Review, 36*(1), 44–62. http://doi.org/10.1080/02796015.2007.12087951

Figlio, D. N., & Getzler, L. S. (2002). *Accountability, ability, and disability: Gaming the system* (Working paper 9307). National Bureau of Economic Research Digest. https://www.nber.org/system/files/working_papers/w9307/w9307.pdf

Fleischman, H. L., Hopstock, P. J., Pelczar, M. P., & Shelley, B. E. (2010). *Highlights from PISA 2009: Performance of U.S. 15-year-old students in reading, mathematics, and science literacy in an international context* (NCES 2011-004). U.S. Department of Education, National Center for Education Statistics. https://nces.ed.gov/pubs2011/2011004.pdf

Flono, F. (2011, August 19). Testing, cheating, and failing. *The Virginian-Pilot,* p. 7. https://pilotonline.newsbank.com/doc/news/1393D772DE5B4168

Fordham, S., & Ogbu, J. U. (1986). Black students' school success: Coping with the "burden of 'acting White'." *The Urban Review, 18,* 176–206. https://doi.org/10.1007/BF01112192

Friedman, A. A., & Daniello, F. (2010). Professionalism > politics + policy + pedagogy: The power of professionalism. In A. Stairs & K. Donnell (Eds.), *Research on urban teacher learning: Examining contextual factors over time* (pp. 169–189). Information Age Publishing.

Gallman, S., & Gallagher, D. (2024, June 10). *Louisiana classrooms now required by law to display the Ten Commandments.* CNN Politics. https://www.cnn.com/2024/06/19/politics/louisiana-classrooms-ten-commandments/index.html

Gilligan, C. (1982). *In a different voice: Psychological theory and women's development.* Harvard University Press.

Global Alliance. (2021). *Global Threat Assessment 2021.* Available at https://www.weprotect.org/global-threat-assessment-21/

Goldfeld, S., Woolcock, G., Katz, I., Tanton, R., Brinkman, S., O'Connor, E., & Giles-Corti, B. (2015). Neighborhood effects influencing early childhood development: Conceptual model and trial measurement methodologies from the kids in communities study. *Social Indicators Research, 120*(1), 197–212. https://doi.org/10.1007/s11205-014-0578-x

Green, R. E., Krause, J., Briggs, A. W., Tomislav, M., Stenzel, U., Kircher, M., Patterson, N., Li, H., Zhai, W., Fritz, M. H.-Y., Hansen, N. F., Durand, E. Y., Malaspinas, A.-S., Jensen, J. D., Marques-Bonet, T., Alkan, C., Prüfer, K., Meyer, M., Burbano, H. A., . . . Pääbo, S. (2010). A draft sequence of the Neanderthal genome. *Science, 328*(5979), 710–722. https://doi.org/10.1126/science.1188021

Greene, B. (2004). *The fabric of the cosmos; space, time and the texture of reality.* Knopf.

Greene, D. (2012, February 27), '*Space chronicles': Why space exploration still matters* [Interview]. NPR Books. http://www.npr.org/2012/02/27/147351252/space-chronicles-why-exploring-space-still-matters

Gumbrecht, J., Shoichet, C. E., Sutton, J., Levs, J., & Carter, C. (2013, April 3). *Former Atlanta schools superintendent reports to jail in cheating scandal.* CNN Justice. http://www.cnn.com/2013/04/02/justice/georgia-cheating-scandal/index.html

Haberman, M. (1991). The pedagogy of poverty versus good teaching. *Phi Delta Kappan, 73*(4), 290–294. https://kappanonline.org/the-pedagogy-of-poverty-versus-good-teaching/

Haberman, M. (1995). *Star teachers of children in poverty.* Routledge.

Haberman, M. (2005). *Star teachers: The ideology and best practice of effective teachers of diverse children and youth in poverty.* The Haberman Educational Foundation.

Haberman, M. (2008). *Gentle teaching in a violent society.* Educational Horizons.

Haberman, M. (2010). The pedagogy of poverty vs. good teaching. *Kappan, 92*(2), 81–89.

Haberman, M., Gillette, M., & Hill, D. (2018). *Star teachers of children in poverty.* Routledge.

Haier, R. J., Jung, R. E., Yeo, R. A., Head, K., & Alkire, M. T. (2005). The neuroanatomy of general intelligence: Sex matters. *Neuroimage, 25*(1), 320–327. https://doi.org/10.1016/j.neuroimage.2004.11.019

Hannover, B., & Kessels, U. (2004). Self-to-prototype matching as a strategy for making academic choices: Why high school students do not like math and science. *Learning and Instruction, 14*, 51–67. https://doi.org/10.1016/j.learninstruc.2003.10.002

Hawking, S. 1988. *A brief history of time.* Bantam Books.

Herrnstein, R. J., & Murray, C. (1994). *The bell curve.* The Free Press.

Higgs, R. (2007, March 15). *The trillion-dollar defense budget is already here.* http://www.independent.org/newsroom/article.asp?id=1941

Hill-Jackson, V., Hartlep, N., & Stafford, D. (2019). *What makes a star teacher: 7 dispositions that support student learning.* ASCD.

Hill-Jackson, V., & Stafford, D. (2017). *Better teachers, better schools: What star teachers know, believe and do.* Information Age Publishing.

Hmelo-Silver, C. (2004). Problem-based learning: What and how do students learn? *Educational Psychology Review, 16*(3), 235–266. https://doi.org/10.1023/B:EDPR.0000034022.16470.f3

Hofstadter, R. (1963). *Anti-intellectualism in American life.* Knopf.

Hong, M., & Kang, N. (2010). South Korean and the US secondary school science teachers' conceptions of creativity and teaching for creativity. *International Journal of Science and Mathematics Education, 8,* 821–843. https://eric.ed.gov/?id=EJ896762

Horn, C. (2003). High-stakes testing and students: Stopping or perpetuating a cycle of failure? *Theory Into Practice, 42*(1), 30–41. https://doi.org/10.1207/s15430421tip4201_5

Hotz, R. L. (2005, July 3). Revealing thoughts on gender and brains. *Los Angeles Times.* https://www.seattletimes.com/nation-world/revealing-thoughts-on-gender-and-brains/

Hurd, P. D. (1961). *Biological education in American secondary schools 1890–1960.* American Institute of Biological Sciences.

Idris, D., Joseph, A., John, I., Peris-Mencheta, S., & Rios, E. (2018). *Snowfall* [TV series]. Twentieth Century Fox Home Entertainment.

Karukstis, K. K. (2010). A horizontal mentoring initiative for senior women scientists at liberal arts colleges. *Council on Undergraduate Research Quarterly, 31*(2), 33–39. https://go.gale.com/ps/i.do?id=GALE%7CA247530438&sid=googleScholar&v=2.1&it=r&linkaccess=fulltext&issn=10725830&p=AONE&sw=w&userGroupName=anon%7E29df4211&aty=open-web-entry

Kincheloe, J. L. (2004). *Knowledge and critical pedagogy: An introduction.* Semantic Scholar.

Kind, P. M., & Kind, V. (2007). Creativity in science education: Perspectives and challenges for developing school science. *Studies in Science Education, 43*(1), 1–37. https://doi.org/10.1080/03057260708560225

Koebler, J. (2011, October 13). STEM heavily featured in new "no child" legislation. *US News & World Report.* http://www.usnews.com/news/blogs/stem-education/2011/10/13/stem-heavily-featured-in-new-no-child-legislation

Kohlberg, L. (1958). *The development of modes of thinking and choices in years 10 to 16* [Doctoral dissertation, University of Chicago]. https://www.proquest.com/openview/c503bf59d762abe5818e1b24c484d41a/1?pq-origsite=gscholar&cbl=18750&diss=y

Kolodziej, T. (2011). The benefits and detriments of the No Child Left Behind ct. *ESSAI. 9*(Article 21), 1–5.

Kotler, S. (2012, October 11). Einstein at the beach: The hidden relationship between risk and creativity. *Forbes.* http://www.forbes.com/sites/stevenkotler/2012/10/11/einstein-at-the-beach-the-hidden-relationship-between-risk-and-creativity/

Kozol, J. (2005). *The shame of the nation: The restoration of apartheid schooling in America*. Crown Publishers.

Kupari, P., Välijärvi, J., Linnakylä, P., Reinikainen, P., Brunell, V., & Leino, K. (2004). *NUORET OSAAJAT: PISA 2003—Tutkimuksen ensituloksia. Koulutuksen tutkimuslaitos, Jyväskylän yliopisto* [National report, Institute for Educational Research at the University of Jyväskylä]. www.jyu.fi/ktl/pisa/PISA_2003_-KIRJA_press.pdf

Kwang, N. A., & Smith, I. (2004). The paradox of promoting creativity in Asian classroom: An empirical investigation. *Genetic, Social and General Psychology Monographs, 130*, 307–330. https://doi.org/10.3200/MONO.130.4.307-332

Ladson-Billings, G. (1995). Toward a theory of culturally relevant pedagogy. *American Educational Research Journal, 32*(3), 465–491. https://doi.org/10.3102/00028312032003465

Langdon, D., McKittrick, G., Beede, D., Khan, B., & Doms, M. (2012). *STEM: Good jobs now and for the future* (ESA Issue Brief #03-11). U.S. Department of Commerce, Economics and Statistics Administration. https://eric.ed.gov/?id=ED522129

Lavin, T., Higgins, C., Metcalfe, O., & Jordan, A. (2006). *Health impacts of the built environment: A review*. Dublin Institute of Public Health in Ireland. https://studylib.net/doc/13623793/health-impacts-of-the-built-environment-a-review

Leary, B. (2005). "Sharp, William (1805–1896)." In *Oxford Dictionary of National Biography*. Oxford University Press.

Lee, J. D. (1998). Which kids can "become" scientists? Effects of gender, self-concepts, and perceptions of scientists. *Social Psychology Quarterly, 61*, 199–219. https://doi.org/10.2307/2787108

Lee, J. (2002). More than ability: Gender and personal relationships influence science and technology involvement. *Sociology of Education, 75*(4), 349. https://doi.org/10.2307/3090283

Leeman, Z. (2022, October 24). *CNN's Brianna Keilar challenges Biden education secretary on declining student performance—He admits it's a 'wake up call.'* CNN. https://www.mediaite.com/tv/cnns-brianna-keilar-challenges-biden-education-secretary-on-student-declines-report-and-he-admits-its-a-wake-up-call/

Lienesch, M. (2007). *In the beginning: Fundamentalism, the Scopes Trial, and the making of the antievolution movement*. University of North Carolina Press.

Lim, H. J. (2010). *A longitudinal investigation of reading in high-stakes tests for adolescent English language learners* [Doctoral dissertation, University of Southern California]. ProQuest. https://eric.ed.gov/?q=birth+AND+rates+AND+distributions&pg=2&id=ED516383

Lim, W., & Plucker, J. A. (2001). Creativity through a lens of social responsibility: Implicit theories of creativity with Korean samples. *Journal of Creative Behavior, 35*, 115–130.

Locke, G. (2011, July 14). *STEM jobs help America win the future*. The White House Blog. http://www.whitehouse.gov/blog/2011/07/14/stem-jobs-help-america-win-future

Locurto, C. (1991). *Sense and nonsense about IQ: The case for uniqueness*. Greenwood Publishing.

Loftus, M. (2012). Brighter outlook: Community colleges find that faculty-student research projects help spot and develop STEM talent. *ASEE Prism, 21*(8), 36–39.

Lubienski, S. T., & Lubienski, C. (2005). A new look at public and private schools: Student background and mathematics achievement. *Phi Delta Kappan, 86*(9), 696–699.

Lupanov, A. (2013). *Sensational discovery: NEFU scientists have discovered a female mammoth*. North-eastern Federal University. http://www.s-vfu.ru/en/news/detail.php?SECTION_ID=&ELEMENT_ID=12458#

Madaus, E., & Clarke, M. (2001). The adverse impact of high stakes testing on minority students: Evidence from 100 years of test data. In G. Orfield & M. Kornhaber (Eds.), *Raising standards or raising barriers? Inequality and high stakes testing in public education*. The Century Foundation.

Malcolm, S. (1997). *Girls succeeding in mathematics, science and technology: Who works and what works* [Paper presentation]. American Association of University Women Conference Proceedings, Philadelphia, PA.

Malik, T. (2010). *NASA grieves over cancelled program*. NBC News. https://www.nbcnews.com/id/wbna35209628

Malinas, G., & Bigelow, J. (2012). "Simpson's paradox." In E. N. Zalta (Ed.), *The Stanford encyclopedia of philosophy* (Fall 2012). https://plato.stanford.edu/archives/sum2016/entries/paradox-simpson/

Mangan, K. (2012, November 2). Despite efforts to close gender gaps, some disciplines remain lopsided. *Chronicle of Higher Education*, B4–B6.

Manouchehri, A. (2004). Implementing mathematics reform in urban schools: A study of the effect of teachers' motivation style. *Urban Education, 39*(5), 472–508.

Mansfield, C., (2023). STS-135: The Final Voyage. NASA News and Events Website, 4/19/2023. https://www.nasa.gov/missions/space-shuttle/sts-135/sts-135-the-final-voyage/

McKinney, S., Bol, L., & Berube, C. (2010). Mathematics teaching with the stars. *2010 Yearbook of Urban Learning, Teaching and Research*, 36–50.

McKinney, S., Fuller, S., Hancock, S., & Audette, R. (2006). Does "highly qualified" make you a star? *Teacher Education and Practice, 19*(1), 80–93.

McKinney, S., Robinson, J., & Berube, C. (2013). Real teaching in the math classroom. *Teacher Education and Practice, 26*(4), 797–815.

McManamy, J. (2011, October 6). *Steve Jobs—Making connections and creativity*. Knowledge is Necessity. http://knowledgeisnecessity.blogspot.com/2011/10/steve-jobs-making-connections-and.html

McNair, T., Bensimon, E., & Malcom-Piqueux, L. (2020). *From equity talk to equity walk*. Wiley & Sons.

Merrill, N., Waters, T. E., & Fivush, R. (2016). Connecting the self to traumatic and positive events to identity and well-being. *Memory, 24*(10), 1321–1328. http://doi.org/10.1080/09658211.2015.1104358

Mervosh, S. (2022, September 1). The pandemic erased two decades of progress in math and reading. *The New York Times.* https://www.nytimes.com/2022/09/01/us/national-test-scores-math-reading-pandemic.html

Mervosh, S., & Wu, A. (2022, October 24). Math scores fell in nearly every state, and reading dipped on national exam. *The New York Times.* https://www.nytimes.com/2022/10/24/us/math-reading-scores-pandemic.html

Mitchell, R. (1981). *The graves of academe.* Little, Brown & Co.

Misuraca, K., & Hall, M. (2022). One on one with U.S. Secretary of Education. DC News Now; US & World News. https://www.dcnewsnow.com/news/us-and-world/one-on-one-with-u-s-secretary-of-education/#:~:text=%E2%80%9CThe%20results%20released%20today%20from%20the%20National,unacceptable%2C%20and%20a%20reminder%20of%20the%20impact

Morella, M. (2013a, March 18). *Making STEM matter for the next generation of astronauts and engineers.* U.S. News & World Report. http://www.usnews.com/news/blogs/stem-education/2013/03/18/making-stem-matter-for-the-next-generation-of-astronauts-and-engineers

Morella, M. (2013b, January 31). *Many high-schoolers giving up on STEM.* U.S. News & World Report. http://www.usnews.com/news/blogs/stem-education/2013/01/31/report-many-high-schoolers-giving-up-on-stem

Morganson, V. J., Jones, M. P., & Major, D. A. (2010). Understanding women's underrepresentation in science, technology, engineering, and mathematics: The role of social coping. *The Career Development Quarterly, 59,* 169–179.

Nam, J. (2024, September 23). Most diverse colleges in the US. *Best Colleges,* 2–24. https://www.bestcolleges.com/resources/most-diverse-colleges/

National Archives and Records Administration. (n.d.). *Brown v Board of Education.* http://www.ourdocuments.gov/doc.php?flash=true&doc=87

National Assessment of Education Progress. (2022). Available: Participate in NAEP | NAEP (ed.gov)

National Center for Education Statistics. (2012). *The nation's report card: Science 2011* (NCES 2012-465). Institute of Education Sciences, U.S. Department of Education. https://nces.ed.gov/nationsreportcard/pdf/main2011/2012465.pdf

National Center for Educational Statistics. (2023). Fast Facts. https://nces.ed.gov/fastfacts/index.asp?faq=FFOption3#faqFFOption3

National Center for Education Statistics. (n.d.). *Executive Summary.* http://nces.ed.gov/pubs/web/96184ex.asp

National Council of Teachers of Mathematics. (2000). *Principles and standards of school mathematics.*

National Education Association. (1894). *Report of the Committee of Ten on secondary school studies with the reports of the conferences arranged by the committee.* The American Book Company.

National Education Association. (2021, April 9). *President Biden calls for historic investment in Title I.* National Education Association.

National Education Association. (2024, March 11). *President Biden calls for historic investment in Title I.* National Education Association. Available: President Biden's FY2025 Budget prioritizes students, educators, and public schools | NEA.

National Research Council. (2011). *Successful K–12 STEM education: Identifying effective approaches in science, technology, engineering, and mathematics.* National Academies Press.

National Science Foundation. (n.d.). http://www.nsf.gov/index.jsp#1

Nation's Report Card. (2022). *Long term trend (LTT) mathematics and reading assessments at ages 9 and 13.* nationsreportcard.gov

New York City Department of Education. http://schools.nyc.gov/TeachNYC/who/default.htm

Nisbett, R. E. (2003). *The geography of thought: How Asians and Westerners think differently... and why.* Free Press.

Office of Management and Budget. (2000). Standards for defining metropolitan and micropolitan statistical areas [Notice]. *Federal Register, 65*/249, 82228–82238. https://www.federalregister.gov/documents/2000/12/27/00-32997/standards-for-defining-metropolitan-and-micropolitan-statistical-areas

Packard, B. (1999, April 19–23). *A 'composite mentor' invention for women in science.* Paper presented at the American Educational Research Association Annual Meeting, Montreal, Quebec, Canada.

Palmer, R., Ryan, D., Moore III, J., & Hilton, A. (2010). A nation at risk: Increasing college participation and persistence among African-American males to stimulate U.S. global competitiveness. *Journal of African-American Males in Education, 1*(2), 105–124.

Park, L., Young, A., Troisi, J., & Pinkus, R. (2011). Effects of everyday romantic goal pursuit on women's attitudes toward math and science. *Personality and Social Psychology Bulletin, 37*(9), 1259–1273. https://doi.org/10.1177/0146167211408436

Parker, S. (2013, April 25). Charter Schools vs. Public: Is one better than the other? New data shows just how well kids are doing in many of the nation's charter schools. *Takepart.* http://www.takepart.com/article/2013/04/25/charter-schools-are-they-better-public-schools.

Parolin, Z., Collyer, S., & Curran, M. A. (2022). *Absence of monthly child tax credit leads to 3.7 million more children in poverty in January 2022.* Columbia University Center on Poverty and Social Policy.

Payton, F. (2004). *Making STEM careers more accessible. Black Issues in Higher Education, 21*(2), 90. https://eric.ed.gov/?id=EJ701839

Pennsylvania State Education Association. (2024). *Biden vs. Trump on education.* psea.org/news—events/Publications/voice-november-2020/biden-vs.-trump-on-education/

Perie, M., Grigg, W., & Dion, G. (2005). *The nation's report card: Mathematics, 2005* (NCES 2006-453). U.S. Department of Education, National Center for Education Statistics. https://nces.ed.gov/nationsreportcard/pdf/main2005/2006453.pdf

Phillips, S. E. (2009). High-stakes testing accommodations: Validity versus disabled rights. *Applied Measurement in Education, 7*(2), 93–120. https://doi.org/10.1207/s15324818ame0702_1

Platz, C. (2012). Igniting women's passion for careers in STEM. *Techniques: Connecting Education and Careers, 87*(4), 26–29. https://eric.ed.gov/?id=EJ985284

Poplin, M., Rivera, J., Durish, D., Hoff, L., Kawell, S., Pawlak, P., Hinman, I., Straus, L., & Veney, C. (2011). She's strict for a good reason: Highly effective teachers in low performing urban schools. *Phi Delta Kappan, 92*(5), 39–43. https://eric.ed.gov/?id=EJ917640

Prado-Galbarro, F. J., Pérez-Ferrer, C., Ortigoza, A., López-Olmedo, N. P., Braverman-Bronstein, A., Rojas-Martínez, R., de Castro, F., & Barrientos-Gutiérrez, T. (2021). Early childhood development and urban environment in Mexico. *PloS One, 16*(11), e0259946. https://doi.org/10.1371/journal.pone.0259946

Proctor, A., & Lupiani, J. (2024). *Atlantic public schools cheating scandal: Remaining defendants make deals to avoid prison.* Fox 5 Atlanta News. https://www.fox5atlanta.com/news/atlanta-public-schools-cheating-scandal-defendants-court

Ramey-Gassert, L., & Schroyer, M.G. (1992). Enhancing science teaching self-efficacy in pre-service elementary teachers. *Journal of Elementary Science Education, 4,* 26–34.

Ravitch, D. (2010a, August 1). *Obama's race to the top will not improve education.* Huffpost. http://www.huffingtonpost.com/diane-ravitch/obamas-race-to-the-top-wi_b_666598.html

Ravitch, D. (2010b). *The death and life of the great American school system: How testing and choice are undermining education.* Basic Books.

Rebhorn, L. S., & Miles, D. D. (1999). High-stakes testing: Barrier to gifted girls in mathematics and science? *School Science & Mathematics, 99*(6), 313–319.

Reveles, J. M., Cordova, R., & Kelly, G. J. (2004). Science literacy and academic identity formulation. *Journal of Research in Science Teaching, 41*(10), 1111–1144. https://doi.org/10.1002/tea.20041

Rillero, P. (2010). The rise and fall of science education: A content analysis of science in elementary reading textbooks of the 19th century. *School Science and Mathematics, 110*(5), 277–286.

Roberts, D. (2023, April 8). *The closing of the Floridian mind.* Flaglerlive.com. https://flaglerlive.com/closing-floridian-mind/#google_vignette

Roberts, S., Zhang, A., Morgan, R., & Musu-Gillette, L. (2016). *Indicators of school crime and safety: 2015* (NCJ Number: 249758). U.S. Department of Justice. https://bjs.ojp.gov/library/publications/indicators-school-crime-and-safety-2015

Robinson, D., & Lewis, C. (2017). Typologies for effectiveness: Characteristics of effective teachers in urban learning environments. *Journal of Urban Learning, Teaching, and Research, 13*, 124–134. https://files.eric.ed.gov/fulltext/EJ1150198.pdf

Rommes, E., Overbeek, G., Scholte, R., Engles, R., & De Kemp, R. (2007). 'I'm not interested in computers': Gender-based occupational choices of adolescents. *Information, Communication and Society, 10*, 299–319. https://doi.org/10.1080/13691180701409838

Rosser, S. V., & Taylor, M. Z. (2009). *Why are we still worried about women in science?* American Association of University Professors. http://www.aaup.org/AAUP/pubsres/academe/2009/MJ/Feat/ross.htm

Rumberger, R. W. (2011). *Dropping out: Why students drop out of high school and what can be done about it.* Harvard University Press.

Russell, M., & Kavanaugh, M. (2011). *Assessing students in the margin: Challenges, strategies and techniques.* Information Age Publishing.

Sadker, M., & Sadker, D. (1995). *Failing at fairness: How America's schools cheat girls.* Macmillan.

Sampson, Z. C. (2012, May 11). Va. 8th-graders show improved science ability. *The Virginian-Pilot*, p. A3.

Sapna, C., & Plant, V. (2010). Explaining underrepresentation: A theory of precluded interest, *Sex Roles, 63*, 475–488. https://doi.org/10.1007/s11199-010-9835-x

Saunders, B. E., & Adams, Z. W. (2014). Epidemiology of traumatic experiences in childhood. *Child and Adolescent Psychiatric Clinics of North America, 23*(2), 167–184. https://doi.org/10.1016/j.chc.2013.12.003

Sawyer, R. K. (2006). *Explaining creativity.* Oxford University Press.

Schiebinger, L. (1993). *Nature's body: Gender in the making of modern science.* Beacon Press.

Science of Gender and Science. (2005, May 12). *Pinker vs. Spelke: A debate.* Harvard University. http://www.edge.org/3rd_culture/debate05/debate05_index.html

Sehgal, N., & Smith, G. (2009). *A religious portrait of African-Americans.* Pew Research Center's Forum on Religion & Public Life. https://www.pewresearch.org/religion/2009/01/30/a-religious-portrait-of-african-americans/

Sherkat, D. E. (2011). Religion and scientific literacy in the United States. *Social Science Quarterly, 92*(5), 1134–1150. https://doi.org/10.1111/j.1540-6237.2011.00811.x

Simeone, A. (1987). *Academic women: Working towards equality.* Bergin & Garvey Publishers.

Shomaker-Dimeo, P., et al. (2023). House republican budget threatens public education and opportunity for young people. *American Progress.* https://www.americanprogress.org/article/house-republican-budget-threatens-public-education-and-opportunity-for-young-people/#:~:text=The%20 bill%20would%20eliminate%20funding,existing%20resource%20 and%20achievement%20gaps. Accessed May 28, 2025.

Soares, D. A., & Vannest, K. J. (2013). STEM project-based learning and teaching for exceptional learners. In R. M. Capraro, M. M. Capraro, & J. R. Morgan (Eds.), STEM project-based learning: An integrated science, technology, engineering, and mathematics (STEM) approach (pp. 85–98). SensePublishers. https://doi.org/10.1007/978-94-6209-143-6_10

Somashekhar, S., & Nakamura, D. (2012, February 27). Rick Santorum takes heat for 'snob' comment against President Obama. *The Washington Post.* http://www.washingtonpost.com/politics/rick-santorum-takes-heat-for-snob-comment-against-president-obama/2012/02/27/gIQADiXteR_story.html

Sparks, S. (2021, March 31). *Data: What we know about student mental health and the pandemic.* Education Week. https://www.edweek.org/leadership/data-what-we-know-about-student-mental-health-and-the-pandemic/2021/03

Steele, C. M. (1997). A threat in the air: How stereotypes shape intellectual identity and performance. *American Psychologist, 52*(6), 613–629. https://doi.org/10.1037/0003-066X.52.6.613

Steele, C. M., & Aronson, J. (1995). Stereotype threat and the intellectual test performance of African Americans. *Journal of Personality and Social Psychology, 69*(5), 797–811. https://doi.org/10.1037/0022-3514.69.5.797

Sterling, D. (2007). Modeling problem-based instruction: A health-science investigation put students in the role of epidemiologists. *Science and Children, 45*(4), 50–53.

Sterling, D., & Hargrove, D. (2012). Is your soil sick? *Science and Children, 49*(8), 51–55.

Sterling, D., Matkins, J. J., Frazier, W., & Logerwell, M. (2007). Science camp as a transformative experience for students, parents, and teachers in the urban setting. *School Science and Mathematics, 107*(4), 134–147. https://doi.org/10.1111/j.1949-8594.2007.tb17928.x

Tan, E., & Calabrese-Barton, A. (2008). From peripheral to central: The story of Melanie's metamorphosis in an urban middle school science class. *Science Education, 92*(4), 567–590. https://doi.org/10.1002/sce.20253

The Guardian (2025, June 5). *Judge blocks Trump's ban on Harvard's foreign students from entering the US.* Harvard University. https://www.theguardian.com/education/2025/jun/05/harvard-trump-foreign-student-ban. Accessed June 7, 2025.

The White House. (n.d.-a). *Fact sheet: President Biden announces new actions to advance racial and educational equity on 70th anniversary of Brown v. Board of education* [Press release]. https://www.whitehouse.gov/briefing-room/statements-releases/2024/05/17/fact-sheet-president-biden-announces-new-actions-to-advance-racial-and-educational-equity-on-70th-anniversary-of-brown-v-board-of-education/

The White House. (n.d.-b). *Reforming No Child Left Behind.* https://obamawhitehouse.archives.gov/issues/education/k-12/reforming-no

-child-left-behind#:~:text=NCLB%20has%20created%20incentives%20for,schools%20that%20miss%20their%20goals

Todd, B. (2023, August 8). *6-year-old boy who shot teacher later boasted about it, affidavit says*. CNN. https://transcripts.cnn.com/show/cnc/date/2023-08-08/segment/12

Tolley, K. (1996). Science for ladies, classics for gentlemen: A comparative analysis of scientific subjects in the curricula of boys' and girls' secondary schools in the United States, 1794–1850. *History of Education Quarterly, 36*(2), 129–153. https://doi.org/10.2307/369502

Tosun, T. (2000). The beliefs of preservice elementary teachers toward science and science teaching. *School Science and Mathematics, 100*(7), 374–379.

Turner, J. C., Hogg, M. A., Oakes, P. J., Reicher, S. D., & Wetherell, M. S. (1987). *Rediscovering the social group: A self-categorization theory*. Basil Blackwell.

Underhill, O. E. (1941). *The origins and development of elementary-school science*. Scott, Foresman and Company.

U.S. Department of Education. (2009). *Race to the top program executive summary*. https://files.eric.ed.gov/fulltext/ED557422.pdf

U.S. Department of Education. (2022, October 27). *Remarks by U.S. secretary of education Miguel Cardona on nation's report card*. https://www.ed.gov/about/news/speech/remarks-us-secretary-of-education-miguel-cardona-nations-report-card

U.S. Department of Education. (n.d.). *Science, technology, engineering, and math: Education for global leadership*. https://www.ed.gov/media/document/stem-overviewpdf

U.S. Department of Education. (2024, February 24). *Fact sheet: U.S. Department of Education releases 2023 update to equity action plan, outlines new commitments to advance equity*. https://www.ed.gov/news/press-releases/fact-sheet-us-department-education-releases-2023-update-equity-action-plan-outlines-new-commitments-advance-equity#:~:text=202)%20401%2D1576%2C-,press%40ed.gov,-The%20U.S

United States Military Academy at West Point. (n.d.). *History of West Point*. https://www.westpoint.edu/about/history-of-west-point

United States Office of Management and Budget. (2012). *Budget of the U.S. Government, Budget of the United States Government, Fiscal year 2013*. United States Government. http://www.gpo.gov/fdsys/search/pagedetails.action?packageId=BUDGET-2013-BUD

Van De Walle, J., Karp, K., & Bay-Williams, J. (2023). *Elementary and middle school mathematics: Teaching developmentally*. Pearson.

Virginia Initiative for Science Teaching and Achievement, George Mason University. http://vista.gmu.edu/

VISTA Science Education Faculty Academy, George Mason University, May 21–25, 2012, http://vista.gmu.edu/

Waterman, A. S. (2020). "Now what do I do? ": Toward a conceptual understanding of the effects of traumatic events on identity functioning. *Journal of Adolescence, 79*(1), 59–69. http://doi.org/10.1016/j.adolescence.2019.11.005

Weinstein, D. (2008). *Herbert Spencer*. Stanford Encyclopedia of Philosophy. http://plato.stanford.edu/entries/spencer/

West, M., & Curtis, J. W. (2006). *AAUP faculty gender equity indicators 2006*. American Association of University Professors. https://www.aaup.org/NR/rdonlyres/63396944-44BE-4ABA-9815-5792D93856F1/0/AAUPGenderEquityIndicators2006.pdf

Yager, R. E. (2000). The history and future of science education reform. *The Clearing House, 74*(1), 51–54. https://doi.org/10.2307/30189634

Yale Faculty Committee. (1828). *1828 report*. https://www.yale.edu/sites/default/files/files/1828_curriculum.pdf

Yore, L. D., Pimm, D., & Tuan, H. L. (2007). *The literacy component of mathematical and scientific literacy*. International Journal of Science and Mathematics Education, 5(4), 559–589. https://doi.org/10.1007/s10763-007-9089-4

Zimmer, C. (2013, March 3). Interbreeding with Neanderthals: Telltale evidence of ancient liaisons with Neanderthals and other extinct human relatives can be found in the DNA of billions of people. *Discover Magazine*. https://www.discovermagazine.com/planet-earth/interbreeding-with-neanderthals

APPENDIX

Notes Concerning the Teaching of Physics to Elementary/ Secondary Students

There are some basic concepts that a teacher should be able to transmit to students concerning the physics of gravity, space, and time. These require no mathematics at this level, and are relatively easy to comprehend. Teaching physics at the conceptual level for the general public is the best way to get students of all ages interested in science. I have had great success teaching physics this way to both college non-science majors and middle school students. One of the points of this book is to actualize the teaching of high level STEM subjects to real students in real classrooms across America. This reading list is provided for those inclined to read further on these topics. These books were written by scientists for regular people with no scientific backgrounds, in easy to understand formats. These books are not recent publications, but I can find no better ones. These authors have more recent publications but these books listed are powerful tools for lay people to understand physics.

Reading List

Brian Greene

1999: *The Elegant Universe: Superstrings, Hidden Dimensions, and the Quest for the Ultimate Theory*
2005: *The Fabric of the Cosmos: Space, Time, and the Texture of Reality*
2008: *Icarus at the Edge of Time* (This is a children's book)
2011: *The Hidden Reality: Parallel Universes and the Deep Laws of the Cosmos*

Stephen Hawking

1988: *A Brief History of Time*
1993: *Black Holes and Baby Universes and Other Essays*
2001: *The Universe in a Nutshell*
2002: *On the Shoulders of Giants*
2005: *A Briefer History of Time*
2005: *God Created the Integers: The Mathematical Breakthroughs That Changed History*
2010: *The Grand Design*

Children's Books Co-Written With His Daughter Lucy
2007: *George's Secret Key to the Universe*
2009: *George's Cosmic Treasure Hunt*
2011: *George and the Big Bang*

Michio Kaku

2008: *Physics of the Impossible*
2011: *Physics of the Future*

Websites

For teaching string theory to K–12 students:

NOVA Teachers: Elegant Universe; the Einstein's Dream http://www.pbs.org/wgbh/nova/education/activities/3012_elegant.html (Includes a 33 page teacher's guide. Most activities align with the National Science Education Standards Physical Science standard, Structure of Atoms and Structure and Properties of Matter sections).

NOVA Teachers: The Science of Superstrings http://www.pbs.org/wgbh/nova/education/activities/3012_elegant_00.html

Videos

These videos will aid in the teacher's understanding, as well as the students.

NOVA: The Elegant Universe, Brian Greene http://www.pbs.org/wgbh/nova/physics/elegant-universe.html

Making Sense of String Theory, TED Talks, Brian Greene http://www.youtube.com/watch?v=YtdE662eY_M

About the Author, Co-Author, and Contributor

Dr. Clair T. Berube is associate professor and chair of the department of education at Virginia Wesleyan University. Dr. Berube previously taught education and science education courses at Hampton University. She is the PI of the Robert NOYCE grant from the National Science Foundation that recruits and trains mathematics, chemistry, earth and environmental science, and biology majors to become STEM teachers in urban high-needs schools. Dr. Berube taught middle school science in Norfolk Public Schools, where she won a teaching award. She has published articles and books on education and science education. Dr. Berube has also taught for the University of Virginia interdisciplinary studies program.

The Robert Noyce scholarship program is a National Science Foundation initiative to increase the number of competent and highly-trained STEM teachers in America's high-need schools.

Robert Noyce was one of the co-founders of the Intel Corporation in 1968. Silicon Valley is so named because of the silicon chip, which Noyce is credited with inventing. The NOYCE foundation was founded in 1991 by his family, and funds STEM education in K–12 schools, as well as higher education teacher training grants. It is a very valuable way to recruit and train energetic young people to become science teacher leaders of tomorrow (Robert Noyce, pbs http://www.pbs.org/transistor/album1/addlbios/noyce.html).

Dr. Sueanne McKinney was a retired associate professor of education at Old Dominion University, and formerly assistant professor of mathematics education at ODU. Dr. McKinney has numerous publications concerning urban and mathematics education. She has created partnerships with several high-poverty urban public schools in the Norfolk Public School system, where she makes a huge difference in the daily lives of children. Dr. McKinney has also worked on several grants concerning STEM education in urban schools. Dr. McKinney taught middle school mathematics, also in Norfolk Public Schools, before becoming a college professor. She has won numerous teaching awards.

We would both like to thank Norfolk Public Schools for giving us our start and vision for education.

* * *

Kala Burrell-Craft is an associate professor in the educational leadership program at the University of Maryland Eastern Shore. Dr. Burrell-Craft is the former director of a 100% grant funded teacher residency program at her former university, which she grew into a nationally recognized program that received the 2022 American Association of Colleges for Teacher Education's Best Practice for Multicultural Education and Diversity award. She co-leads the School of Education college-wide initiatives centered on justice, equity, diversity, and inclusion as a member of the university JEDI committee. Her research interests are related to identity development, educational spaces (urban and rural), antiracist teacher and leadership preparation (culturally responsive pedagogy), critical literacies (CRT), and social justice. Dr. Burrell-Craft has multiple publications in peer-reviewed journals and has been awarded over eight million dollars in grants. She is a graduate of the Leadership and Mentoring Institute (LMI) Class of 2022, the award recipient of the American Association of Blacks in Higher Education's 2024 Early Career Award, and a proud active member of Alpha Kappa Alpha Sorority, Inc.

www.ingramcontent.com/pod-product-compliance
Lightning Source LLC
Chambersburg PA
CBHW050540300426
44113CB00012B/2195